# MANAGING YOUR NONPROFIT FOR RESILIENCE

# TED BILICH

# MANAGING YOUR NONPROFIT FOR RESILIENCE

## USE LEAN RISK MANAGEMENT TO IMPROVE PERFORMANCE AND INCREASE EMPLOYEE ENGAGEMENT

WILEY

Published by John Wiley & Sons, Inc., Hoboken, New Jersey.
Published simultaneously in Canada.

For general information on our other products and services or for technical support, please contact our Customer Care Department within the United States at (800) 762-2974, outside the United States at (317) 572-3993 or fax (317) 572-4002.

Wiley also publishes its books in a variety of electronic formats. Some content that appears in print may not be available in electronic formats. For more information about Wiley products, visit our web site at www.wiley.com.

*Library of Congress Cataloging-in-Publication Data:*

Names: Bilich, Ted, author.
Title: Managing your nonprofit for resilience : use lean risk management to
   improve performance and increase employee engagement / Ted Bilich.
Description: Hoboken, New Jersey : John Wiley & Sons, Inc., [2023] |
   Includes bibliographical references and index.
Identifiers: LCCN 2022032945 (print) | LCCN 2022032946 (ebook) | ISBN
   9781394153824 (cloth) | ISBN 9781394153848 (adobe pdf) | ISBN
   9781394153831 (epub)
Subjects: LCSH: Nonprofit organizations—Management. | Risk management.
Classification: LCC HD62.6 .B566 2023  (print) | LCC HD62.6 (ebook) | DDC
   658/.048—dc23/eng/20220826
LC record available at https://lccn.loc.gov/2022032945
LC ebook record available at https://lccn.loc.gov/2022032946

Cover Design: Wiley
Cover Image: © Retouch man/Shutterstock

SKY10037996_110722

*To Jennifer, my love and my best friend. With Coqui, we make a great pack.*

# Contents

*Preface*                                                                  *ix*

*Acknowledgments*                                                          *xi*

        **Introduction**                                    1

Chapter 1   You and Your Nonprofit Deserve Risk
            Management                                         3

Chapter 2   Learn the Language of Lean Risk Management   17

**Part I**      **Identify**                                  **35**

Chapter 3   Perform a Risk Inventory                        37

**Part II**    **Prioritize**                                **49**

Chapter 4   Prioritize Your Risks                           51

Chapter 5   Create Your Risk Register                       61

**Part III    Respond**                                            **71**

Chapter 6   Respond to Your Risks                                    73

**Part IV    Assess and Improve**                                  **95**

Chapter 7   Develop a Risk Management Cycle                         97

Chapter 8   Work with Risks at the Board Level                     107

Chapter 9   Implement Lean Risk Management
            Incrementally                                          115

            Conclusion                                             129

Appendix 1  50 Reasons Why It Is Hard to Run a Nonprofit           131

Appendix 2  Questions to Use During Risk Inventories               147

Appendix 3  Nonprofit Risk Management Policy Templates             171

Appendix 4  Fundamental Risk Management Elements
            (FRaMEs)                                               175

Appendix 5  A Simple Compliance Checklist                          181

*Sources and Methodology*                                          187

*Notes*                                                            197

*About the Author*                                                 209

*Index*                                                            211

# Preface

WHAT IF NONPROFITS could avoid crises and devote more resources to the causes they want to advance?

What if instead of being merely reactive, nonprofits could be proactive—confronting issues with radical candor, then taking reasonable steps to address their most important challenges?

What if nonprofits could create virtuous cycles of action, leading team members to think like owners and strive for continuous improvement?

What if, instead of being fragile (susceptible to reversals) or merely robust (strong, but unyielding), nonprofits could actually become *resilient*: able to bounce back from challenges and spring forward to create and take advantage of opportunities?

I have spent decades exploring these questions. I have trained hundreds of nonprofits and gathered data every step of the way. This book is the result of those efforts.

# Acknowledgments

THIS BOOK WOULD not have happened without the support and encouragement of Linda Lenrow Lopez. She has been a thought partner on these concepts and, just as important, one of my dearest friends. Risk Alternatives may have lost her to the Wikimedia Foundation, but the world is a better place for her being the risk management principal at that critical bastion defending the accumulation and sharing of information.

In addition to Linda, I want to thank everyone who reviewed and commented on earlier drafts of this work, especially Jennifer Adams, Amy Coates Madsen, Jan Young, Jenny Palazio, and John Ottenhoff. Scott Schaefer, Greg Wolfson, Michael Brown, and Miriam Cleeman were instrumental in helping me choose the right way to package these concepts in evocative ways. Thanks, as well, to Heather Angel and Laura Hurt, who do so much to keep Risk Alternatives running at peak performance. At Wiley, thanks to Brian Neill, Debbie Schindlar, and Susan Geraghty, who have made production of this book a fun experience.

I also want to thank the hundreds of nonprofits who contributed data to our survey database, participated in our workshops and webinars, and permitted us to serve them as advisors. I want to thank all the members of Nonprofits Build Strength Together (BeST). I stand in awe of the work you do every day. I want to thank the scores of funders who have supported our work in communities around the United States. Finally, special thanks to Fred Brown, Hannah Karolak, and Emma Yourd from The Forbes Funds; Kevin Dean, Andrea Hill, and Annie Schmitz from Momentum Nonprofit Partners; Amy Coates Madsen and Kate Hull from Maryland Nonprofits; and Keith Timko and Xander Subashi from The Support Center for Nonprofit Management. You have been thought partners in helping to develop resources that make nonprofits better. Together we can make the nonprofit sector so much stronger.

# Introduction

THIS BOOK AIMS to help nonprofits not only survive but also thrive. The aim is not just to avoid fragility, where uncertainty can shake a nonprofit to its core. It is not even mere robustness, where the nonprofit can survive shocks because it is cautious, solid, and stable.

This book instead aims to build nonprofit resilience—an ability to bounce back from setbacks and spring forward toward opportunities. To that end, this book provides nonprofits with a blueprint for creating an early warning system to help a team see downside and upside risks and take reasonable steps to address them.

# 1

---

# You and Your Nonprofit Deserve Risk Management

NONPROFITS PLAY A vital role in communities around the world.

In the developing world, nonprofits often serve as the only barrier between life and death. Even in highly developed economies, however, nonprofits provide enormous impact. In the United States, for instance, nonprofits provide nearly 6 percent of the gross domestic product. They provide just under one out of every ten US jobs, and they comprise half the nation's hospitals, almost half the institutions of higher education, close to 80 percent of vocational rehabilitation facilities, and approximately 80 percent of daycares. Furthermore, they account for almost all operas and orchestras, one out of every five nursing homes, and about one third of private clinics and home health care facilities.[1]

Impressive as those figures are, they understate the importance of nonprofits in our communities. Nonprofits often provide essential goods and services for those who are most vulnerable. They address the needs of those who, because of age, health, socioeconomic status, or power dynamics, cannot operate effectively on their own in our economy. If the US economy is an engine, nonprofits are its vital lubricant. Nonprofits reduce friction, helping the otherwise sharp edges of society function more safely, productively, and humanely.

Nonprofits strive for sustainability, growth, and responsiveness to meet their important roles in society. But the harsh truth is that running a nonprofit is hard and getting harder. When addressing most risks, many nonprofit leaders have a limited and linear thought process:

1. Risk is bad.
2. I should avoid risk when I can.
3. I should insure against the risks I can't avoid.
4. I should worry about all the rest.

This book aims to help. The framework for improvement set out in this book is based on effective risk management—a structured process for identifying and dealing with risks before threats become crises and opportunities pass the organization by. By implementing this methodology, nonprofits can increase clarity and peace of mind and find untapped sources of value.

## You should read this book if you are a nonprofit leader or team member, a student, a nonprofit funder, or a nonprofit advisor

This book is written principally for nonprofit leaders. When you see this book refer to you, this book is speaking directly to you. You are being held to increasingly unpredictable standards of care, and you need to understand how to use risk management principles to protect and advance your operations and meet your mission.

This book is also aimed at students learning about nonprofit practice. Nonprofit risk management has long been overlooked in undergraduate and advanced degree programs. This book helps fill that void.

The book is also for funders. When funders place their resources in the hands of a nonprofit, they need to be confident that their investment is sound. A nonprofit without effective risk management is flying blind. Funders have no assurance that nonprofits without effective risk management understand their true capabilities or will perform effectively with donated resources. This is not to say funders know better than nonprofits about what nonprofits should be doing. Instead, funders should understand the language and value proposition of risk management so that they can explore and support this capacity with the grantees they fund.

Finally, this book is written for nonprofit advisors. Attorneys, accountants, and bankers need to be aware of whether their clients are protecting themselves from emerging threats and preparing themselves to seize on potential opportunities. Consultants providing organizational development, leadership training, strategic planning services, or other advice need to consider how those efforts interact with the risk management function. Advisors and consultants can achieve substantial synergies by becoming more aware of what risk management is, why it is important, how it improves operations, and how it is implemented effectively.

## Read the Book Straight Through

This book is designed to be read from start to finish—at least the first time. The Contents recommends a step-by-step approach, and that approach is most effective for nonprofits who are interested in resilience and sustainability. (In fact, the chapter titles and subheadings of this book are designed to tell a story about your success.)

The book begins by explaining why risk management is important (this chapter) and identifying core vocabulary (Chapter 2). It then describes how you can perform a risk inventory to identify threats and opportunities throughout your nonprofit (Chapter 3). The book then explains how to prioritize your risks (Chapter 4) and develop your first risk register—the prioritized punch list of the most important issues facing your organization (Chapter 5). Chapter 6 then notes the basic ways you can respond to a risk (a much broader repertoire than merely avoiding, insuring, and worrying). The book then explains how to expand your resilience efforts by developing a risk cycle (Chapter 7), getting your board involved (Chapter 8), and building out a powerful process over time (Chapter 9).

At the conclusion of each chapter, you will find an "Insight and Exploration" section. These optional materials can help you reflect on what you read, apply it to your own experience, and find resources that would provide further practical guidance.

In addition to the text, the book provides several useful appendixes. Appendix 1 helps you persuade skeptics that nonprofits need risk management by noting many of the challenges that nonprofits face. Appendix 2 provides hundreds of questions you and your team can use to uncover risks in each functional area of your nonprofit and the context in which it operates. Appendix 3 sets out two examples of risk management policies that you can use as templates. Appendix 4 supplies a list of policies and processes that support risk management efforts. And Appendix 5 provides a simple compliance checklist that you can use when evaluating that function.

Finally, this book includes an extensive bibliography. The intent is to provide you with the source materials that shaped this book and additional materials that may guide your resilience journey.

## Nonprofits Are Vulnerable

Even in the best of times, the nonprofit business model is extremely challenging. Imagine this story. A friend of yours comes to you with a business proposition. She says she wants you to invest your retirement money in her new business. It will have a few notable characteristics:

- To perform some of its basic services (including much of its marketing and customer service), the business will often rely on volunteers.
- The business will be criticized if it ever consistently makes more money than it spends annually.
- No matter how effective its operations may be, many people will judge the business based on how much overhead it has—in other words, how much money it spends on its people and other assets rather than directly providing services.
- The business will have no access to capital markets. It will be unable to sell stock to fund long-term initiatives. Instead, it will have to rely on government grants and the kindness of strangers to provide donations to make ends meet.
- If it sells products or services, it will sell them at below-market rates.
- The business will hire at below-market rates and put its employees in challenging circumstances, where they deal with customers who may be under substantial stress or hardship.

No one would invest their retirement savings in this kind of a business. But this book just described the average social services nonprofit in the United States. You might object that this is a caricature, but most nonprofits have at least some of those characteristics, any one of which creates imminent peril and unique challenges.

In fact, the nonprofit business model is so ridiculously challenging that an early draft of this chapter used 25 pages describing 50 different reasons why it is tough to run a nonprofit. Early readers loved the material but were overwhelmed by the reality of these frustrations. They knew the model is demanding, and so do you. In a compromise with your sanity, this book moves those reasons to Appendix 1. If anybody ever doubts that nonprofits need to focus on resilience and sustainability, refer them to that appendix.

In short, nonprofits have a wacky business model. Pandemics, political and social unrest, racial reckoning, and a host of other issues only compound the difficulties.

## Heeding Experts, Nonprofits Are Beginning to Explore Risk Management

Nonprofit risk management is a consensus best practice. One leading nonprofit support organization, Independent Sector, speaks of a nonprofit board's obligation "to review regularly the [nonprofit's] need for general liability and directors' and officers' liability insurance, as well as take other actions necessary to mitigate risks."[2] The notes accompanying this standard are even more explicit: "board members of a charitable organization are responsible for understanding the major risks to which the organization is exposed, reviewing those risks on a periodic basis, and ensuring that systems have been established to manage them."[3]

Other authorities agree. The Standards for Excellence Institute, whose benchmarks have been adopted for use in many states and national organizations, similarly states that "organizations should make every effort to manage risk and periodically assess the need for insurance coverage in light of the organization's activities and its financial capacity."[4] *The Principles & Practices for Nonprofit Excellence* (originally adopted by the Minnesota Council of Nonprofits and since by many other states) echo that "nonprofits should periodically assess their risks, take appropriate actions to minimize those risks and purchase appropriate levels of insurance to wisely manage their liabilities."[5]

The District of Columbia Bar advises that "every nonprofit organization needs to create a risk management plan and review it annually."[6] And the Human Services Council of New York states that nonprofit "boards, in conjunction with staff, must be engaged in risk assessment and implement financial and programmatic reporting systems that enable them to better predict, quantify, understand, and respond appropriately to financial, operational, and administrative risks."[7]

Most nonprofits have gotten the message to one extent or another. Risk Alternatives LLC has asked hundreds of nonprofits the following survey question: "Is risk management a regular topic of conversation at your staff meetings?" Here are the responses:

- 18% respond "Yes, we raise and address risk management issues specifically and regularly."
- 32% respond "We don't have a formal process but raising and discussing risks is a normal part of our staff meeting agendas."
- 34% respond "Sometimes. We discuss risks when we see them."
- 14% respond "Rarely. We tend to focus on the immediate needs of our service population(s)."

Finally,

- 3% respond "Never. We do not discuss risks."[8]

These responses show that most nonprofits are beginning to heed the call to implement risk management into their operations. Those that do not are increasingly out of step with their peers.

## Nonprofit Risk Management Standards Are Tightening Because of Increased Social Distrust

Larger organizations in the private sector have adopted risk management on the heels of 20 years of financial gyrations and allegations of corporate mismanagement. The Basel II accords, adopted by the Basel Committee on Banking Supervision in 2001, provided banks with specific guidance about operational risk practices, supervision of those practices, and necessary disclosures about risk.[9] In 2004, the Committee of Sponsoring Organizations of the Treadway Commission (COSO) released the *Enterprise*

*Risk Management—Integrated Framework,* which provided a thorough framework for helping corporate management understand and apply risk management principles.[10] In 2009, the International Organization for Standardization adopted ISO 31000, another framework for dealing with risk management.[11] In 2010, the US Securities Exchange Commission adopted regulations requiring disclosures by publicly traded companies about risk management.[12]

This push for risk management and compliance in the private sector stems from worries about accountability and management of "other people's money." Corporations use shareholder proceeds to do things that they could not do without such investments. As a result, regulators reasoned, corporations need to take precautions about what they do with that money and need to provide transparency about those efforts.

Nonprofits also use "other people's money." Nonprofits persuade donors to provide resources that can be funneled toward people or causes in need of attention. Unsurprisingly, they too have faced greater scrutiny in the wake of scandal:

- In March 2016, the Wounded Warrior Project fired its CEO and COO after news reports alleged wasteful spending.[13]
- In January 2016, Goodwill Industries of Toronto declared bankruptcy after facing an "acute cash crunch," leading its CEO and board of directors to "resign . . . en masse."[14]
- In late 2014, the largest social services agency in New York, the Federation Employment and Guidance Service (FEGS), failed suddenly, leading to substantial public soul-searching by regulators and observers.[15]
- In January 2020, New York City filed suit against Childrens Community Services alleging a "massive fraud" in the provision of homeless services.[16]

The threat to nonprofits is real. In a 2015 survey, the second highest concentration of employee thefts occurred in the nonprofit sector (trailing only the financial sector).[17] According to an investigative report published in the *Washington Post* in 2013, during a five-year period more than 1,000 nonprofits in the United States disclosed that they had suffered a "significant diversion" of assets, including "theft, investment fraud, embezzlement and other unauthorized uses of funds."[18]

When trust in nonprofits is imperiled, nonprofits need to make every step count.

## New Technologies Mean New Threats—Especially for Nonprofits

Nonprofits are ill-equipped to address emerging cyber issues. In 2015, for example, the Utah Food Bank announced that 8 percent of its donors (more than 10,000 individuals) may have been affected by a data breach that exposed donor names, addresses, credit card information, and credit card security codes.[19] Nonprofits have been "slower to adapt to the threat environment and allocate their often scarce resources to cyber preparedness and protection" than for-profit and government entities, despite repeated warnings "to understand the risks posed by cyber breaches and data hacks, to engage their boards and leaders on these issues, and to allocate funds and resources to cybersecurity."[20] Unfortunately, in an increasingly high-tech economy, nonprofits are at a disadvantage. Technology often requires significant capital, and nonprofits do not have the same access to capital resources as their for-profit peers.

## The Hidden Jobs of Nonprofit Leadership Drive Leaders to Distraction

Ask most nonprofit advisors about the duties of an executive director or CEO (this book uses the terms interchangeably), and they will tell you the leader is responsible for setting direction, ensuring execution of necessary operations, gathering resources (through fundraising and other development activities), serving the nonprofit's intended beneficiaries, and acting as an ambassador to stakeholders and community.

Behind that accepted description, however, lies a set of hidden jobs—tasks the leader must accomplish one way or another to succeed. Unfortunately, leaders lack practical tools to handle these many hidden tasks, which tend to be addressed, if at all, using half-measures and coping mechanisms. Consider the following:

- The leader must identify, track, and address threats before they become crises.
- The leader must identify, track, and address opportunities to improve existing operations or develop new initiatives to help the organization.
- The leader must focus their own attention and team attention on the most important issues currently facing the organization.
- The leader must energize team members to take responsibility and accept accountability for identifying and dealing with threats and opportunities as part of their daily activities.
- The leader must regularly and reliably elicit information from team members about their worries, fears, and hopes.
- The leader must motivate their board to focus their limited time and energy on the most constructive engagement for the nonprofit.

In short, nonprofit leaders are tasked with ensuring that their organizations are resilient—that they avoid unforced errors, take advantage of opportunities, bounce back from setbacks, and maximize their impact given a host of constraints.

Coping with these important hidden tasks leads to unnecessary stress, worry, and burden. Psychologists speak of generalized anxiety disorder, which is the pressing sense of worry, anxiety, nervousness, tension, restlessness, inability to sleep, distraction, irritation, fatigue, and rumination that undermines a sufferer's performance and quality of life. You may not personally experience these symptoms, but if you do, you are not alone. Many nonprofit leaders find themselves in a perpetual state of anxiety—and "chronic worry is debilitating."[21] As Joan Garry writes, "Nonprofits can cause a person to transform into someone they don't recognize. Why? Because nonprofits are messy. It's inherent in the formula of the unique beast we call a 501(c)(3)."[22]

## This Book Provides Relief—and a Way Forward

This book aims to reduce nonprofit leaders' anxiety and improve organizational resilience. If you apply the learning in the chapters that follow, you will gain the following:

- **Clarity**, as your nonprofit gains a better understanding of the range of threats and opportunities it faces
- **Identification of low-hanging fruit**—important threats and opportunities that may be addressed with little expenditure and enormous potential return
- **Engagement**, as team members feel that they are rewarded for speaking up to identify and address risks
- **Commitment**, as team members develop a greater appreciation of the interrelationship of different functions within the nonprofit
- A solid **basis for short-term actions**, as the process identifies and prioritizes pressing issues
- A strong **foundation for long-term planning**, as the organization develops a greater understanding of the context in which it operates, including its current and potential reach

If you begin using the tools described in this book, you will gain immediate value. If you stick with them over time, that value will deepen and your organization will improve. You will manage not just for survival but also for resilience.

The challenges described on the preceding pages should not make you feel overwhelmed or want to give up. In fact, hesitation in the face of a compelling need for decisive change is the most dangerous act of all. Effective risk management enables an organization to act with increased confidence and resolve, aware of threats and alert to opportunities. It carries a message of hope and empowerment. That's the promise of this book. You can think about the described processes as cognitive therapy for you and your organization—applied organizational mindfulness.

## Insight and Exploration

1. How many of the vulnerability factors described in the section called "Nonprofits Are Vulnerable" apply to your nonprofit?
2. Look at Appendix 1. How many of the issues identified there apply to your nonprofit?
3. Does your state have a list of nonprofit best practices? (Google "nonprofit best practices" or "nonprofit standards.")
4. How would you answer the survey question in the section called "Heeding Experts . . ."? How do you think your staff would answer the question? In other words, how confident are you that your team knows how your nonprofit currently performs risk management?
5. Even nonprofits that do not have risk management processes in place still use tools and best practices that support risk management objectives. For instance, most nonprofits have a strategic plan, an employee handbook, job descriptions, and insurance. This book terms these other tools of resilience *fundamental risk management elements*, or FRaMEs. These FRaMEs do not constitute a risk management process on their own, but they decrease the chance of bad things happening or mitigate the potential bad effects. You can read more about those FRaMEs in Appendix 4.
6. Nonprofits are in the crosshairs. As a sign of these times, while this book was being prepared for publication, the *New York Times* published an item asking, "Are you familiar with wrongdoing among nonprofit groups? The *Times* is looking into mismanagement and poor oversight at nonprofits." The newspaper noted that one of their investigative reporters "wants [reader] suggestions about what to dig into next."[23]
7. When one nonprofit engages in mismanagement or misconduct that causes public outcry, every nonprofit suffers, because donors

lose faith, suffer disillusionment, and feel less likely to engage in helping behaviors.[24] As a result, one reason to enhance risk management and resilience in your own nonprofit is that your behavior affects others' results.

8. Beth Kanter and Allison Fine explore related issues of nonprofit vulnerability in their book *The Smart Nonprofit*.[25] As technology increasingly permits organizations to access and use "big data" to gather operational and strategic insights, nonprofits face numerous technical and ethical challenges. *The Smart Nonprofit* provides recommendations about how nonprofits can grapple with these challenges and advance their missions during times of bewildering technological advances.

9. With respect to the hidden jobs of nonprofit leaders, consider the following:
   a. How do you track threats right now? How do you make sure that everyone who needs to know about those threats is kept informed?
   b. Do you have a method for tracking and exploiting new opportunities? How do you make sure everyone is on the same page so that you can keep abreast of trends and implement continuous innovation?
   c. How do you determine what the most important issues are in your nonprofit? How do you gather input to ensure you are seeing everything you need to see? What criteria do you apply to prioritize issues?
   d. What tools do you currently use to energize team members to take responsibility and accept accountability for identifying and addressing threats and opportunities?
   e. How do you regularly elicit information about risks from team members?
   f. How do you ensure that members of your actively focus on the most important issues facing your nonprofit?

10. When considering whether to implement the practices in this book, consider the value you place on clarity. Research suggests anxiety and lack of clarity impede performance by making people less focused, more irritable, more disengaged, more fearful, and less socially engaged.[26] Conversely, organizational

clarity "appears to be strongly correlated with performance and can act as a leading indicator of future performance."[27]

11. As an additional factor when approaching the book's recommendations, consider the value of employee engagement. Employee engagement is strongly associated with profitability and performance. Employees who feel heard are "4.6 times more likely to feel empowered to perform their best work" and highly engaged teams "show 21% greater profitability" over time.[28]

# 2

# Learn the Language of Lean Risk Management

WHEN PEOPLE USE the term *risk* in everyday conversation, they often mean the possibility of a negative outcome. One mentions the risk associated with catching the flu, drunken driving, or walking across the street without looking both ways.

Some academics and risk management professionals similarly define risk as "a state of uncertainty where some of the possibilities involve a loss, injury, catastrophe, or other undesirable outcome (i.e., something bad could happen)."[1] This book disagrees. Because the language of risk can be confusing, this book will define *risk*, *risk management*, and its favored approach, *Lean Risk Management*.

## Risk Involves Threats *and* Opportunities

This book advises a holistic approach to risk. Risk is neither good nor bad. Risk is simply an acknowledgment that none of us can see into the future and predict exactly what will happen, our concession to the fact that we are human. Thus, as used in this book, risk "is any deviation from the expected. Defined this way, risk includes both downside and upside volatility."[2] (See Figure 2.1.)

| Vocabulary |
| --- |
| Risk = Uncertainty |
| Threat = Negative risk |
| Opportunity = Positive risk |

Figure 2.1   Core Vocabulary

If the concept of "upside risk" seems foreign, consider financial investments. We expect a lower rate of return from a money market account than a stock mutual fund. Because the stock mutual fund is a collection of securities, each of which could go up or down in value, we expect greater volatility but also greater potential return.

We hope that the mutual fund manager has chosen the collection of securities that, on balance, will appreciate. We understand that this might not be the case. We make the investment *because* there is risk, and we have some expectation of return that is commensurate with that risk.

This book uses the term *threat* when talking about potential negative events or consequences. A threat is something that could go *wrong*.

This book uses the term *opportunity* when talking about potential positive events or consequences. Whether it is a new initiative, changing a process or policy, entering into a joint venture, increasing staffing in a particular function, or enhancing the training and development of existing staff, an opportunity is something that could go *right*. An opportunity is an uncertainty that presents upside volatility.

In many large organizations, a risk management process focuses almost exclusively on threats. Large organizations often devote significant budgets to identify and mitigate threats, but they may also have entire separate departments, such as research and development and strategic planning, devoted to positive potential risks. Thus, when larger organizations speak of *risk management*, they often mean *loss prevention*.

Although classifying risk management as synonymous with threat management may make sense when an organization is large enough to have substantial resources and divisions of labor, smaller, leaner organizations do not have that luxury. Thus, nonprofits beginning to implement Lean Risk Management are best served by considering risk and risk management as dealing with both upside and downside uncertainties for at least three reasons:

- Most nonprofits have some intuitive sense that they need to worry about things that could go wrong. Relatively few, however, use "positive worry" to think about what might go **right** and how to increase the likelihood of good things happening.
- Even nonprofits that engage in brainstorming, strategic planning, and visioning exercises often fail to record and follow up on such sessions. As a result, nonprofit leaders may tend to get captured by the tyranny of what is happening now instead of laying the groundwork for future expansion and growth.

- In selling risk management to your team, your board, and your stakeholders, you will gain greater traction if you emphasize hope as well as worry. People do not like to look under rocks and think about what might go wrong. By contrast, most people like to think about the upside.

## Risk Management Involves Commitment, Process, Information, and Action

If risk is uncertainty, risk management is about addressing that uncertainty. More specifically, as used in this book, **risk management is a commitment to a regular process of gathering credible information about threats and opportunities and acting on the most important risks faced by an organization.**

### Risk Management Involves a Commitment

Risk management involves a commitment by senior leadership and board members to have an organization identify threats and opportunities as a regular part of daily operations. Risk management does not mean casting an occasional eye toward uncertainty but rather thinking about the potential consequences of activities as a matter of routine.

### Risk Management Involves a Process

Risk management is not something that can be done once in an exercise and never revisited. It is instead a dynamic series of actions involving the adoption of systems, controls, policies, and procedures over time, then periodic evaluation of those steps to achieve better results. This does not mean that risk management is complex or requires enormous effort; to the contrary, the principles are simple and the effort is relatively minor. But it does mean that risk management is ongoing rather than static.

### Risk Management Involves Information

Individually, people are not very good at gathering information or evaluating that information. However, by gathering more than one viewpoint, considering additional sources, and systematizing the way we evaluate, we can accomplish tremendous feats of risk analysis.

### Risk Management Involves Action—Taking Steps to Assert Control

Risk management is not passive but rather emphasizes active effort to address threats and opportunities.

## Comparisons and Contrasts Help Clarify Risk Management

To gain a better idea of what risk management is, consider what risk management is *not*.

### Risk Management Is Not Worrying

Risk management is the opposite of worrying, which is giving way to anxiety or unease. A nonprofit does not adopt risk management to fret or construct worst-case scenarios. Effective risk management programs do not freeze an organization or inhibit it from accomplishing its goals.

To the contrary, effective risk management helps an organization exercise informed judgment to manage its environment, control what it can control, take advantage of opportunities that are worth pursuing, and achieve its goals. Risk management decreases worry because senior leadership is more aware of the potential consequences of the nonprofit's actions. Rather than fretting about the issues that lurk under every rock, you can instead make informed decisions based on greater awareness of your organization and its environment.

## Risk Management Is Not Strategic Planning

Because risk management uses the language of threats and opportunities, some nonprofit executives may be inclined to believe that risk management is synonymous with strategic planning. No doubt, most nonprofits have gone through strategic planning processes in which they have performed a SWOT analysis, which looks at strengths, weaknesses, opportunities, and threats. But risk management and strategic planning are distinct. Strategic planning projects into the future what an organization would like to accomplish. Risk management focuses on identifying threats and opportunities within the current environment so that the nonprofit can accomplish its goals.

Although much work has been done over the past decade to improve nonprofit strategic planning, most strategic planning is usually static, or at best episodic. A nonprofit engages an outside consultant to create a strategic plan. The strategic plan projects objectives into the future (usually three or five years) and may map out performance benchmarks along the way. Some strategic planning processes end there: planners believe that by identifying objectives, they have provided value by creating a common sense of direction within the organization. Some strategic planning processes go further, revisiting the strategic plan periodically to assess progress and, if necessary, modify either the goals or the methodologies for achieving those goals.

By contrast, risk management emphasizes creating a dynamic process for identifying and addressing threats and opportunities as they arise within an organization. Risk management focuses on creating processes and procedures that energize all levels of an organization to be alert to issues that might affect operations and impact mission. Effective risk management strives to create a "learning organization," where employees are taught to ask questions, admit uncertainties, acknowledge mistakes, and improve every aspect of the organization over time.

Think of it this way. Effective strategic planning determines what mountains a nonprofit intends to scale, what metrics will be used to determine when the nonprofit has reached the summit, and what milestones will determine progress during the ascent. Risk management focuses on preparedness and effective orienteering along the path. Before scaling the mountain, you must determine your capabilities and fitness for the journey. You must set out with proper equipment and regularly scan the horizon for threats and opportunities. You must focus on the critical few truly important issues that may stand in your way or allow you to vault forward. Without effective risk management, a "strategic plan" is merely a strategic hope.

## Risk Management Is Not Auditing

Some nonprofit executives believe that risk management is closely related to annual auditing. This misconception can arise in at least two contexts. First, they may believe that an organization does not need a risk management program because it undergoes annual financial audits. Second, they may believe that the auditing process performed by accountants is synonymous with risk management. Both beliefs are dangerously misguided.

Financial audits are performed by accountants. They are performed to provide reasonable assurance that a nonprofit's financial statements are presented in accordance with generally accepted accounting principles. Nonprofits get annual audits either because they have reached a stage of income at which some regulatory authority demands annual audits, or they have funders who demand independent audits to have some outside verification of a nonprofit's assets, liabilities, and cash flows.

Annual financial audits, however, are not the same as risk management. The purpose of an independent financial audit is not to identify threats and opportunities for an organization. Independent financial audits are performed solely for the purpose of providing some outside verification of the financial condition of the nonprofit. Auditors will routinely provide a "management letter" to a nonprofit at the conclusion of an audit that identifies any material weaknesses in the financial reporting functions uncovered during the audit. They will sometimes provide additional notes and guidance about any other operational issues they see during their audit. But auditors do not take on the responsibility of identifying risks throughout an organization. Having an annual audit in no way excuses an organization from having a risk management program. Any organization that took that approach would place itself in peril.

Some nonprofits also have an internal audit function, which focuses on making sure an organization is following its processes. This internal audit function provides a useful supplement to risk management, but it generally does not create a process for identifying, prioritizing, and responding to threats and opportunities.

### Risk Management Is Not (Just) Insurance

Insurance and risk management are not synonymous. Insurance is one part of an effective risk management program, because it is one way of shifting certain threats to a third party (see Chapter 6). But for at least four reasons, for all but the smallest and newest nonprofits, insurance cannot be the only risk management approach:

- **Risk management efforts can reduce the need for insurance and reduce its cost.** The theory of risk management is to identify potential threats and take steps to reduce the likelihood or impact of those threats. Sound risk management can reduce the chances of identified risks coming to fruition. Risk management can reduce the magnitude of exposure. It can often reduce the speed at which potential problems turn into claims.
- **Insurance never covers an entire loss.** Deductibles, co-pays, damage caps, and other limitations reduce the value of the insurance relative to the claim presented. Furthermore, to the extent that a claim results in litigation, the out-of-pocket costs of that litigation may not be covered by an insurance policy. Even if the litigation attorney's fees and costs are covered, an insured faces substantial costs in terms of business disruption. And rarely does any form of insurance cover the reputational cost of claims against an organization.

- **There are other ways to shift risk of loss.** An insurance policy is basically an agreement in which both sides are making a wager. You, as the insured, are hedging against the possibility that a claim will arise. The insurer is betting that, on average, few enough claims of the sort insured against will arise that the premiums, invested responsibly, will cover the company's exposure and create profits. As a potential insured, one has other ways to hedge against a threat. To the extent the threats involve business relationships (e.g., employment, purchase or sale of goods or services), much of the risk can be identified and addressed through sound contracting practices. Other threats may be reduced by entering into a joint venture, partnering, or consortium arrangements with others. Still other threats may be reduced by seeking and employing expert counsel (e.g., law, accounting).

- **Despite professions about being "a good neighbor," standing "on your side," putting you "in good hands," insurance companies are in the business to make money.** They make money by collecting premiums, investing that money, and avoiding the payment of claims to the greatest extent consistent with business ethics and the law. This means that any insurance policy will be subject to certain exclusions. It also means that the insured must carefully disclose all pertinent information in an insurance application. It is unsound business for an insurer to generously overlook exclusions or statements in an insurance application that could be read, in hindsight, to be less than fully candid. In other words, when the time comes to make a claim, never assume that an insurer is looking out for your organization. Only you can do that—through sound risk management.

## Risk Management Is Not a Crystal Ball

A risk management program does not attempt to catalog and address every possible threat and opportunity. No reasonable organization could ever achieve such omniscience, and it is fruitless and wasteful to try. As Nassim Nicholas Taleb has persuasively argued in his book *The Black Swan*, every organization faces the possibility of a black swan—an event that is outside the realm of regular expectations and yet has an enormous impact.[3] But even ignoring extreme events, no organization can create a risk management program that identifies and addresses every possible risk. Risk management involves committing reasonable resources to be more aware of a nonprofit's environment and then taking steps to address the uncertainties within that environment.

Rather than thinking of risk management as a crystal ball, a better metaphor is a lamp in the darkness. A lamp does not enable the traveler to see around corners or deep into pits. A lamp cannot prevent something harmful from sneaking up behind the  traveler, nor does it generate the volition that impels the traveler on their journey. But a lamp can help the traveler identify hazards, avoid pitfalls, and perhaps find tools and paths along the way. Furthermore, as its light fades off into the distance, a lamp may provide the traveler with a healthy reminder of the limits of what can be seen, so that they choose their course with due care and mindfulness.

## Three Powerful Tools Drive Risk Management: The Inventory, Register, and Cycle

Risk management emphasizes three basic tools: the risk inventory, the risk register, and the risk cycle.

A **risk inventory** is a process of looking for threats and opportunities. As described in later chapters, a risk inventory enables your team to identify risks within every function of the organization, as well as threats and opportunities presented by the external environment.

A **risk register** is a tool for prioritizing those risks, assigning them to responsible parties, and following up. It is best to keep it simple: an organization should use a basic spreadsheet listing the particular risk, its priority, who is responsible for the risk, the next step the organization intends to take, and the date by which that action should be taken.

As the team discovers new information or takes steps to address a particular risk, a given risk may change priority and therefore go up or down on the list. Other threats or opportunities may be added. Some risks may be removed altogether as the organization deals with them. By gathering all these moving parts in a single document, the risk register provides a nonprofit with a dynamic, prioritized punch list of high-value items that deserve attention.

A **risk cycle** implements regular check-ins to drive home within your staff the fact that risk management is a regular part of business. These regular inquiries provide opportunities for team members to identify new risks, prioritize them, take steps in response, and then assess those risks in light of the responses.

A nonprofit does not engage in a single risk management project. Instead, effective risk management includes incorporating the identification, prioritization, response, and improvement steps into the organization's standard operating procedures. This is graphically demonstrated in Figure 2.2.

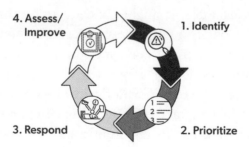

**Figure 2.2   The Risk Cycle**

## Identify

A successful nonprofit organization identifies threats and opportunities across its different functional areas. Initially, it does so through the risk inventory exercise just mentioned. Later, it hones that process by adding components that feed risk identification into the risk management process more organically, including feedback mechanisms for employees, donors, service recipients, and others.

## Prioritize

When everything is important, nothing is important. Thus, the next step in effective risk management is to prioritize threats and opportunities so that the organization understands its most important issues. As noted, an initial prioritization leads to the nonprofit's first risk register.

## Respond

Having identified threats and opportunities and prioritized them, the organization then makes decisions about how to respond.

The nonprofit may decide to **research and measure** certain risks to understand them better.

It may adopt policies and procedures to **avoid** certain threats altogether. For example, it might cancel activity that creates too many threats, adopt and post safety procedures, create safeguards that force an activity to be performed in a certain way, adopt a nondiscrimination policy, or adopt a whistleblower procedure to protect employees who come forward with their concerns.

The nonprofit may take steps to **mitigate** potential threats. It might fix a sidewalk to prevent injury, adopt a reserve policy to build a financial cushion, or implement nonprofit training for employees to perform tasks in a safer and more effective way.

It may take other steps to **develop** opportunities identified through risk management efforts, such as beginning new initiatives or changing established procedures to achieve greater effectiveness.

The nonprofit may also **shift** its risk to other parties using insurance, joint ventures, or contract language that changes the nature of its interactions.

Finally, a nonprofit may decide to simply **monitor** a risk to observe what happens over time, perhaps applying some trigger criteria to indicate a need to act.

## Assess and Improve

After identifying, prioritizing, and responding to certain threats and opportunities, risks will remain. That's the nature of a nonprofit or any other organization. Because you cannot predict the future, you will always face uncertainty. Yet, effective risk management includes self-reflection to determine whether you can improve the organization's performance:

- How are the policies and procedures working in practice?
- Have our mitigation efforts been effective, and could they be improved through modification?
- Are we developing opportunities effectively, and do we have in place a methodology for identifying new opportunities?
- Have our risk-shifting activities accomplished their task in a cost-effective manner?

After responding, assessing, and improving, an organization does not rest. Instead, it continues to identify, prioritize, respond, and improve, and in doing so, it creates virtuous cycles of strength and resilience.

If you have a process for regularly identifying risks, prioritizing them, and dealing with them, and do that repeatedly according to some agreed cadence, you have a risk management process.

Although some large organizations may spend millions of dollars on risk management, the underlying process is the same when a nonprofit begins that journey on a smaller scale. Behind any potential complexity rests a simple question. How can we become increasingly aware of what is going on around us, including what we think might happen in the future, so that we can take the next reasonable step in the present moment to respond?

## Now Add *Lean* to Risk Management

This book explains that risk analysis goes hand in hand with continuous process improvement, a term popularized by the Lean management movement. Lean arose out of work by Toyota Motor Company to do more with less during the early years after World War II. When Toyota caught up with and then surpassed US auto manufacturers in the early 1980s, academics and business leaders began evaluating and documenting what made Toyota different.[4] John Krafcik first referred to these practices as *lean* in 1988.[5] Since then, Lean practices have spread not only within manufacturing but also throughout service industries.[6]

As Jon Miller and his coauthors put it, Lean businesses strive to advance "a set of core beliefs, including . . . engaging the total workforce, servant leadership, visualization of the real condition of things, respect for people, appreciation for standards, scientific problem-solving, alignment of purpose not only with customers but also with broad stakeholders, curiosity, humility, and a view to the long term."[7]

This book advocates a Lean Risk Management approach for five reasons.

First, when properly performed, risk management is **incremental and iterative**. You perform a cycle, then check to see how the system responds. You do not devote an enormous amount of nonprofit resources initially, and you never spend more than you need. Instead, you take it one step at a time. You use the three tools previously described—the risk inventory, risk register, and risk cycle—to build the capacity you need over time. This incremental, data-driven approach is the essence of Lean.

Second, risk management is not a senior management job. Rather, it involves **energizing an entire workforce** to identify and deal with risks as a part of everyday operations. The Lean in Lean Risk Management emphasizes shared accountability and staff empowerment.

Third, as in Lean, a **relentless focus on the customer should drive every risk management decision**. When this book uses the term *customer*, it means end users of your nonprofit's goods and services: students, patients, service participants, beneficiaries, and so on. Given that nonprofits are always pushed to do more with less, Lean principles and methods provide a reasoned basis for nonprofit operations. Nonprofits provide value to customers through what Lean practitioners would call a value stream—a series of steps a nonprofit performs to satisfy a customer need. Nonprofits should aim to provide **exactly what the customer wants, when they want it, and with a minimum of waste**. The customer's real needs must drive every decision:

- How do we currently provide value to the customer?
- What value do we really provide?
- How do we really know what the customer wants?
- What factors threaten or impede the stream of activities that lead to providing that value to the customer?
- What waste can be trimmed from the value stream to improve performance?
- What opportunities are available to improve our performance?
- What incremental changes can we provide right now that will provide more value to the customer?
- What long-term changes should we consider that would add customer value?

These value-stream questions, drawn from Lean methodology, create powerful rubrics for guiding risk management decisions.

Fourth, **most threats and opportunities that need to be managed are internal** to organizations. By training to become radically aware of what the nonprofit currently faces, then taking measurable, incremental steps in response to those risks, nonprofits can achieve remarkable transformations over time. Lean principles, methods, and tools provide detailed guidance for this continuous process improvement.

But finally, and just as important, **Lean emphasizes investments in resilience and sustainability** to serve clients and communities more effectively over time. Thus, a Lean approach to risk management fits within a broader philosophy about nonprofits. Nonprofits need to be there for the long haul. The best risk management involves sustained investment in the nonprofit training and support of your team. Lean Risk Management is all about building better nonprofits.

## Insight and Exploration

1. What elements of Lean management, if any, do you currently apply in your nonprofit?
2. The value stream analysis described in this chapter is often a crucial reframe for nonprofits. Nonprofits have many customers (beneficiaries, funders, internal stakeholders), and considering values streams forces a nonprofit to begin exploring what each "customer" group actually needs. For more information about value stream analysis, read Karen Martin and Mike Osterling's *Value Stream Mapping*.[8]
3. A nonprofit's customers include their donors, who provide money to the nonprofit with the hope and expectation that the nonprofit will take certain actions. Even when donors give unrestricted money, they still intend that their resources will be wisely spent to further the nonprofit's mission.

4. How many different value streams do you have in your nonprofit? Are the customers the same for each value stream? If not, how do those interests differ, and how do you know that for sure?

5. One way to conceptualize Lean Risk Management is to think of risk management and Lean as hand in glove. Risk management provides a way to identify and prioritize threats and opportunities. Lean provides a method for addressing those risks and engaging in continuous improvement.

# PART

# I

# Identify

*"You absolutely cannot make a series of good decisions without first confronting the brutal facts."*[1]

# 3

---

# Perform a Risk Inventory

YOUR NONPROFIT ORGANIZATION may have great plans, but if you do not have a realistic understanding of your risks, those plans are merely hopes and dreams. Because of this simple truth, the first step in Lean Risk Management should be a risk inventory: a thorough identification of potential threats and opportunities facing the organization. This chapter and the next will explain how.

## You Cannot Figure Out How or Where to Go Until You Know Where You Are Now

A risk inventory is a guided brainstorming exercise to spot potential positive and negative issues within your nonprofit and potential external forces that could affect performance. The benefits of a risk inventory can be substantial:

- **Clarity.** In any organization with more than a few team members, no single person knows everything about the business. Because the risk inventory gathers viewpoints of many participants, it may provide senior management with insight into challenges and opportunities that they may never have seen. Team members within an organization may also gain greater awareness of what others are working on, the challenges others face, and choices faced by senior management.
- **Dialogue and consensus.** The risk inventory process fosters a greater appreciation for different functions within the nonprofit. Team members may find unexpected consensus: many of them may list the same issues within the same functions. Furthermore, when team members disagree about risks, a risk inventory creates a context for important conversations.
- **Commitment.** By showing the joint effort needed to perform risk management, the risk inventory process can increase team commitment to a successful nonprofit risk management process.
- **Ownership.** Each team member who participates in the inventory process comes away with an increased sense of ownership in the nonprofit. The process improves employee engagement and helps team members think like leaders.

- **Small investment, big payoff.** Your first risk inventory should not be exhaustive. It is the initial step toward making risk identification a regular part of your operations. Most risk inventories should take no more than 40 minutes to an hour of individual work for each participant plus 90 minutes to debrief the team on results.

A risk inventory is an invitation to your staff to examine your nonprofit's parts in detail to get a better understanding of the whole.

## A Risk Inventory Is a Simple Orienteering Tool—Here's Your Rule Book

Performing a risk inventory is not challenging. You bring together a small group within your nonprofit, have them perform work independently to identify risks, and then discuss the results.

### *Identify Your Participants*

In small organizations, you may want to include the whole leadership team. Single-person teams might include volunteers, board members, or other stakeholders to provide additional perspectives, but try to keep the initial inventory to staff alone when possible.

In larger organizations, smaller teams typically work better on the first inventory. In a typical nonprofit, we suggest participation by the following personnel:

- CEO/executive director
- Other C-suite staff (particularly the chief financial officer and chief technology officer, if such positions exist in the organization)
- One or two more junior staff (An organization benefits from having at least one junior team member involved, because they may identify issues that have escaped the attention of senior staff.)

The precise composition of your initial risk inventory team will vary depending on the size and nature of your organization. Your guiding principle should be incrementalism. By starting with a small group, you can test how your nonprofit's culture responds to the process and modify your actions going forward.

## Look for Positive and Negative Risks

Recall that risk simply means uncertainty. Risks can be negative or positive, and risk assessment involves both. During your risk inventory, you should identify both threats and opportunities.

## Evaluate All Functions in the Organization

Ask participants to identify threats and opportunities across all functions in the organization, rather than focusing solely on their own areas of expertise. Those outside a function often see threats and opportunities that insiders do not. Consider the following areas (also see Figure 3.1).

**Figure 3.1   Functional Areas of a Nonprofit**

- **Operations.** How your nonprofit performs its programmatic activities
- **Information technology.** The ways your nonprofit uses computers, telephones, and other tools to gather, manipulate, and store data
- **Talent management.** How your nonprofit recruits, trains, supervises, develops, promotes, disciplines, and terminates personnel
- **Finance.** How your nonprofit records and accounts for its operations, reports results, and maintains money and other assets
- **Reputation management.** How your nonprofit is perceived, how it wants to be perceived, and how it attempts to influence perceptions
- **Development.** How your nonprofit raises funds from donors
- **Sales.** How you exchange value for value with your beneficiaries and others (whether or not your nonprofit has a formal sales function)
- **Risk management.** How your nonprofit identifies and addresses threats and opportunities
- **Compliance.** How your nonprofit ensures that it is following internal guidelines and external regulations
- **Planning and visioning.** How your nonprofit creates and tracks its long-term and short-term objectives, how it evaluates performance relative to mission, and how it identifies and adheres to its values
- **Governance.** How your nonprofit's board of directors interacts with staff and how personnel interact with each other
- **Diversity, equity, and inclusion.** How your nonprofit addresses issues relating to race, gender, and inclusivity

You can, of course, vary the functional areas in your initial risk inventory. Most nonprofits, however, benefit from exploring all these areas.

In addition to evaluating these internal functions, participants also evaluate external conditions that may affect the organization. Appendix 2 provides a list of hundreds of questions you can use to stimulate ideas and spot issues not only in the functional areas of the nonprofit but also its external context.

One might reasonably ask why a risk inventory focuses predominantly internally. There are two reasons. First, most areas of greatest threat and opportunity are internal to an organization, not external. Peter Drucker, one of the 20th century's most influential experts on management, noted:

> Efficiency concerns itself with the input of effort into all areas of activity. Effectiveness, however, starts out with the realization that in business, as in any other social organism, 10 or 15 percent of the phenomena—such as products, orders, customers, markets, or people—produce 80 to 90 percent of the results. The other 85 to 90 percent of the phenomena, no matter how efficiently taken care of, produce nothing but costs (which are always proportionate to transactions, that is, to busy-ness).[1]

Drucker made this observation about effectiveness during the 1970s after a career of consulting with some of the most well-respected corporations in the world. Even among those organizations, however, Drucker believed that almost 90 percent of activity was ultimately of relatively little value to the end customers. Contemporary observers skilled in Lean management find the same conditions today; as Carlos Venegas notes, "the proportion of non-value-adding activities in a typical manufacturing firm range from 70 to 95%. In a typical office, non-value-adding activities can be up to 95%."[2] By no means does this suggest that non-value-adding activities are all wasteful and erroneous. Many activities are important even if the customer does not ultimately value them. It does suggest, however, that the internal processes of most organizations—even well-run ones—are areas of fruitful focus.

Moreover, the internal focus of an initial inventory is important because an organization can act decisively only about issues within its control. Your nonprofit can no doubt influence some external forces, but it can materially affect only the functional areas just described. They comprise the principal field of action. In his influential book *The Seven Habits of Highly Effective People*,[3] Stephen Covey used a powerful image involving three concentric circles of potential attention: the outermost Circle of Concern, the middle Circle of Influence, and the innermost Circle of Control. Although you may be vaguely or even profoundly concerned about any number of issues (the Circle of Concern), you can in fact only influence a limited number of those issues (the Circle of Influence). Furthermore, you can control only an even more limited zone of issues (the Circle of Control). Lean Risk Management advises an organization to focus predominantly on those issues that it can control and influence. By focusing on issues within its control, the nonprofit increases its long-term resilience and stability, ultimately expanding its Circle of Control and Circle of Influence.

## Simplify the Process

Instead of having the team search for every single threat and opportunity in each function, make the process more manageable. Ask each team member to identify three threats and one opportunity in each functional area. Have them answer the following questions for each area:

- What are the top three threats that face the nonprofit in this functional area?
- What is the top opportunity for improvement—that is, what change or new initiative would make a material positive impact in the next four months?

In the same manner, have participants identify the top three external issues (positive or negative) confronting the nonprofit.

Have each participant perform their initial work independent from other team members. This helps generate a variety of issues for discussion rather than creating premature consensus that might ignore or hide important results.

## Meet to Discuss Risk Inventory Results

After your team members perform their independent analyses, compile the results. Share them with the team. Meet for discussion, focusing on one functional area at a time, then the external context. In addition, consider the following overarching questions:

- Which function drew the most participant consensus during the independent risk assessments? This functional area may have the greatest potential for short-term results, because the team seems to know what needs attention.
- In which function did the participants identify the greatest number of threats and opportunities? This function may be the area of greatest potential growth.
- In what function did some participants identify many significant issues and feel constrained by the number of risks they could identify while others struggled to identify any at all? The divergence of opinion may suggest that different team members are applying widely different subjective metrics to performance in that area or that some team members do not know much about issues outside their direct responsibility.
- In which function did participants identify the most threats? This function keeps people up at night, which is a key insight for senior management.
- In which functions were the greatest number of opportunities identified? This function might be the organizational sandbox, where team members may want to play.
- Is there consensus about potential external influences, or do views diverge? Having a shared sense of context is critical.

*Important Caveats About an Initial Inventory*

When performing your first risk inventory, keep the following six considerations in mind.

- **You cannot do everything at once.** Your team will find more threats and opportunities than your organization could reasonably address at one time. The next discusses how to prioritize and focus on the most important issues.
- **Some threats and opportunities are not really there.** During an initial risk inventory, participants will list "threats" and "opportunities" that will not withstand scrutiny. No one has all the facts, and personal biases and misinformation could cause your team members to identify false issues.
- **Many issues will need redefinition.** Important issues may be ill-defined. Your team will work toward defining each potential risk so that everyone understands the scope and nature of the issue before you begin developing detailed responses.
- **Your risk inventory is an incomplete list and will change every time you do it.** Your team will not identify every risk facing the organization. Risk is a living, changing force within your nonprofit. By conducting periodic risk inventories, your organization can position itself to strengthen and grow.
- **Expect emotions.** Risk inventories may generate a variety of different emotions. Strong positive emotions are common. Participants may feel energized by their newfound clarity and excited about prospects. They may find that the organization faces fewer issues than they had feared. They may have greater peace of mind because they now know the challenges and opportunities facing the organization. They may feel more appreciated within their functions, and they may appreciate others within the organization more because they understand more about their challenges.

Risk inventories may generate negative emotions, too. An individual may feel frustrated that their complaints are only now being acknowledged. A long list of issues may feel overwhelming. Individuals may feel defensive, particularly when risks lie within their area of expertise. People may also feel uncomfortable identifying risks or problems that stem from others' performance or may want to vent about team members. In light of this dynamic, the leader of the risk inventory initiative may benefit from reviewing a resource on creating constructive conversations, for example, Susan Scott's Fierce Conversations,[4] Karen Martin's Clarity First,[5] or Peter Senge and colleagues' The Fifth Discipline Fieldbook.[6]

Keep in mind, however, that those emotions simmered within your organization before you ever contemplated a risk inventory. Performing the inventory enables your team to surface those important emotions and have important conversations.

■ **Your first risk inventory is just that—an important first step on the path to Lean Risk Management.** Follow up by prioritizing. Do the exercise again in six months. Learn from the differences over time.

## Insight and Exploration

1. Note that the initial inventory is skewed on a 3:1 basis in favor of identifying threats over opportunities. This ratio is based on three intuitions: (1) it is easier for staff to identify things that worry them than things that they would like to change or entirely new initiatives; (2) because the muscle of thinking about improvements and new initiatives needs to be stretched and conditioned, opportunities identified in initial risk inventories are often simply the obverse of threats (e.g., threat— "We face the threat of unauthorized expenditures because we do not require two signatures on checks"—versus opportunity—

"Require two signatures to reduce likelihood of unauthorized expenditures"); and (3) because an initial risk inventory often serves as a form of organizational catharsis, team members approach the project with more thoughts about threats than opportunities.

2. Positive emotions tend to dominate the debriefing sessions. Although people feel some trepidation about the long list of potential challenges, ordinarily the sense of catharsis and clarity far outweigh any disquiet. To improve the likelihood of constructive discussion, consider specifically calling the issue of emotions out when you seek threats and opportunities and again when you distribute the results. Email language such as the following often helps:

[When beginning the inventory:]

When you identify risks, err in favor of speaking up, even if the issue is outside your official duties. In the same way, recognize that others may identify "risks" in your area that are not really there or suggest that you are not doing your job. Rather than being defensive, approach this exercise with an assumption that others are acting in good faith and with constructive intent.

[When distributing the results:]

Remember that participants were asked to err in favor of identifying risks and speaking outside their traditional duties. That means the results of this initial inventory may identify issues that are not really there. Please review the results with a spirit of open-mindedness, rather than defensiveness.

# PART

# II

# Prioritize

"*Almost everything is noise, and a very few things are exceptionally valuable.*"[1]

# 4

## Prioritize Your Risks

Nonprofit risk management requires being honest about what is going on, then taking the next reasonable step in response to that reality. In Chapter 3, we explained how to perform a risk inventory. Now we turn to taking the next reasonable step, which is always a matter of prioritization.

A solid risk inventory exercise will ordinarily identify somewhere between 50 and 100 threats and opportunities across all nonprofit functions. This chapter will explain how to move forward with that list: who should be involved in prioritizing risks, how to prioritize them, and what to do with the results. (See Figure 4.1.)

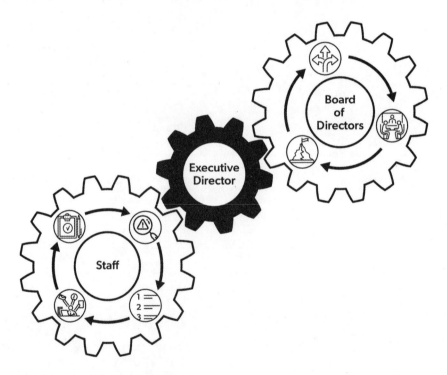

Figure 4.1   The Risk Dialectic

## Prioritization Is a Dialectic

In a for-profit sole proprietorship or closely held corporation, the question of who determines priorities is relatively simple. The organization exists to make money for its owners, so its owners determine the organization's priorities. In most small businesses, the owners are closely associated with day-to-day decisions. The owners may delegate prioritization to one of their members. They may hire someone (a manager or CEO) to make such decisions. Whatever the precise details, however, operational and strategic priorities are determined by and on behalf of the owners.

In a nonprofit organization, however, the question is more complex. Technically, as a matter of nonprofit law, "the organization" decides who weighs in and who makes the ultimate decisions about what is important. "The organization" speaks ultimately through its board of directors, which then delegates execution of the organization's tasks to a CEO or executive director. Thus, in some ways, setting priorities is a matter for boards of directors.

Yet, when considering nonprofit realities, having your board be initially and principally responsible for risk prioritization is unrealistic. Members of nonprofit boards are volunteers: they are unpaid and generally do not put much time into their director activities (at least when compared to staff). The executive director knows dramatically more about the nonprofit than any single board member, and probably knows more about the organization and its activities than all the board members together. The executive director and staff are considerably more engaged than the board in everyday operations. Staff will ordinarily be more aware of the social, community, political, and economic environment relevant to the nonprofit. Thus, in a very real sense, the staff is much more competent than your board when determining priorities.

One way to consider the back and forth of prioritization is the notion of dialectic. In any entry-level philosophy course, you learn about the "dialectic" method of the ancient Greeks, who believed that by focused discussion with people of different experiences and worldviews, one could uncover the truth of matters.

This book advocates an analogous form of dialectic. Staff, board, and executive director all have important perspectives when prioritizing what is most important for the nonprofit.

When beginning nonprofit risk management, therefore, consider the following process for prioritizing issues:

- **Staff involvement first.** Initially, prioritization is a staff function, including the executive director and other key personnel. Staff members know operations, and the staff is aware of the environment in which the nonprofit acts.
- **Executive director evaluation and ranking.** After the staff and executive director perform the initial exercise described in the next section, the executive director makes an independent review of the results to reorder the results as they see fit. After all, the executive director—who is responsible for results—should provide an extra layer of evaluation.
- **Share with the board through the executive director.** After the initial risk inventory identifies a set of priority risks, the results should be shared with the board. At that point, the board should exercise its reasonable, informed business judgment to determine whether those priorities are appropriate. In doing so, the board should probe the executive director about the factual basis for the prioritization. At the same time, the board should recognize that this inquiry is not an invitation to micromanage. The organization hired the executive director to execute on organizational priorities. Execution is not a board activity. As described further in Chapter 8, the board should be inquisitive, even skeptical, but it should leave the operational details and execution to the executive director and staff.
- **Develop dialectic, mediated by executive director.** Over time, of course, priorities may change. As the organization begins to work on various threats and opportunities, some will decrease in priority, and new issues arise. Staff, through the executive director, will keep the board informed of such changes, and the board should weigh in periodically about whether the priorities match the overall direction of the organization. Furthermore, the board may engage in a strategic planning process that modifies operational priorities. You want a healthy push and pull over risk prioritization.

## Use a Simple Method of Prioritization with Your Team

There are many ways to prioritize among competing issues. This book advocates simplicity. After meeting to discuss the results of the risk inventory, each staff participant should take the following steps:

- Each staff member who participated in the risk inventory exercise receives a copy of the results of the exercise—that is, a list of the 100 or so items the team listed as potential risks, threats, or opportunities.
- Each participant is allocated 50 points.
- Each participant allocates those 50 points however they want. They can allocate 50 points to one risk, one point each to 50 items, or any division in between.
- Each participant performs this activity on their own. This is important. You want independent risk assessments.
- After each participant allocates their points, the results are tallied in a master document.

When deciding how to allocate points among various risks, each participant should consider three factors: likelihood, magnitude, and speed of onset. In other words:

- How likely is this risk to manifest?
- If this risk occurs, how large of an impact would it have on the organization?
- If this risk manifests, how much time would the organization have between first noticing the manifestation and bearing the full impact of the risk? What is the risk's lead time?

Plainly, the risk process just described is subjective. Large organizations can spend millions of dollars answering such questions. Except for higher educational and medical institutions, almost no successful nonprofit has the resources to answer any of the questions of likelihood, magnitude, and speed of onset with accuracy and precision. The simpler methodology proposed here enables a team to provide substantial insight into the felt needs of the organization.

## The Leader's Supplemental Prioritization Rubric Provides Additional Input

The prioritization of potential risks during nonprofit risk management is vital to the success of your resilience efforts. A successful nonprofit organization cannot focus on every threat and opportunity; instead, it must focus on the very few issues that must be addressed right now. When you receive the results of a team's initial risk prioritization, you should take steps to ensure that the prioritization reflects a true understanding of the stakes.

The initial prioritization exercise just described enables teams to react emotionally to the nonprofit challenges and risks they face. That is important input because emotions drive attention. But emotions do not tell the whole story. As a result, you should use the following rubric as an additional screen to orient focus toward the most important issues facing the organization.

### Address Immediately

- Legal liability
- Health and safety of employees or customers/clients
- Violation of our values or sound ethical practices

### Address Promptly

- Ambiguity about legal obligations, core values, or sound ethical practices
- Evidence of unhealthy culture
- Exposure to significant reputational harm
- Exposure to significant (for us) financial loss
- Areas of employee complaint or disgruntlement

### Investigate

- Evidence of mission drift
- Evidence of failure to meet plans

- Ambiguity about plans to accomplish mission
- Ambiguity about mission

## Explore

- Areas of potential mission expansion that may serve customers or organizational needs
- Areas of potential new initiatives that fit existing mission
- "Moonshots" that deserve discussion and consideration
- Potential changes to processes that may materially improve performance
- Lack of documented processes
- Inefficient or ineffective processes
- Evidence of lax procedures
- Settled practice, where there is evidence that circumstances have changed

As is evident, this rubric emphasizes that existing legal liability, health and safety violations, and unethical practices should receive prioritization over other identified risks.

Risks that do not trigger concrete, immediate liability, but raise questions about *potential* liability or ethics or value violations, should be prioritized next, along with issues of potential unhealthy culture, reputational harm, significant financial loss, or employee complaints or disgruntlement.

Then come issues that should be investigated as soon as practicable, including concerns about mission drift, execution of strategic or operational plans, or ambiguity about the mission or progress toward mission fulfillment.

Finally, issues of potential upside, performance improvements, or potentially outmoded operations should receive focused exploration.

This rubric can be used by you to place your imprint on staff results from their risk prioritization exercise. Using this tool will enable you to identify the critical few issues that most clearly deserve immediate or prompt attention.

This rubric, moreover, can be used by the entire team to prioritize new risks as they arise after your initial risk inventory.

## Do Not Use Complex Risk Priority Calculations When Starting Out

Many nonprofits want to create a sophisticated calculation of risks—assigning a numeric value for likelihood of occurrence, magnitude of impact, and speed of onset; attempting to quantify the dollar amount of exposure; or even creating some weight-adjusted dollar amount of exposure by multiplying predicted exposure by likelihood. Having a number with multiple underlying calculations appears to provide leadership with comfort that their risk prioritizations are empirically sound, "scientific," and defensible. That approach is inadvisable for many reasons:

- **Different implicit valuations.** Consider the standard 0–10 point scale advocated by many survey creators. Researchers ordinarily label that scale with "not at all likely" over 0, "neither likely nor unlikely" hovering above 5, and "extremely likely" at 10.[1] But what Staff Member 1 means by a 3 will differ from what Staff Member 2 means. And what about the difference between 6 and 7? Moreover, reducing the scale to 0–5 or expanding it to 0–100 will not solve the challenge but rather distort it in different but obvious ways.
- **Different subjective biases.** What Staff Member 1 considers worrisome or feasible and what Staff Member 2 considers worrisome or feasible will vary according to experience and psychological makeup. One staff member may be inherently more risk-averse than another.
- **Overconfidence.** Having a number to compare to another number in a column may create a sense of solidity and certainty that is wholly unjustified. Many people are intimidated by mathematical calculations and reluctant to try to evaluate or

challenge them. The number may therefore take on significance far beyond its trustworthiness.

The numerical exercise advocated in this chapter does not escape issues of implicit valuation differences, subjective biases, overconfidence, or imprecision. Instead, it effectively concedes that initial estimates of risk will be based on human factors that cannot be controlled. The numerical exercise creates a context for discussion about why people view issues differently. The executive director's review and reordering of priorities allows for additional direction and control.

Make no mistake: measurement is extremely valuable. In his insightful book *How to Measure Anything*,[2] Douglas Hubbard provides a road map for helping organizations apply greater precision to their estimates of important uncertainties. He even provides a method for training your team to be better at assessing risks. As your nonprofit develops and hones its risk management process, it is important to invest in greater analytical precision. But such an investment must be considered in light of your budget and your need for precision.

## Insight and Exploration

1. In addition to Hubbard's book, those wishing to avoid number errors may benefit from Sam Savage's *The Flaw of Averages*.[3]

2. Many alternative back-of-the-envelope methods of prioritization are available, including popular rubrics such as the Eisenhower Matrix and others.[4] Feel free to experiment.

# 5

## Create Your Risk Register

PAUSE AND LOOK at your progress:

- You have a greater understanding of the role of nonprofits in their communities.
- You have reflected on the challenges of the nonprofit model and realized that you are not alone in being worried and sometimes distracted by the burdens you face.
- You have learned a basic vocabulary for risk management.
- You have learned how to perform an initial risk inventory, which will provide you with greater awareness and peace of mind about your organization's current needs.
- You have learned a simple process of prioritizing those risks with the input of your team.

This is huge! If you never read another word in this book, you have achieved a tremendous amount!

But more value awaits. You are ready to create your organization's first risk register—one of the simplest and most powerful tools of risk management. This chapter will explain how.

## The Risk Register Is the Key Tool of Lean Risk Management

A risk register is the foundational accountability tool for successful Lean Risk Management and resilience. It is a dynamic list of your nonprofit organization's top potential risks, both threats and opportunities. It provides an up-to-date description of how each risk is defined, who is responsible, what the next step is, and when that step should be completed.

A risk register is critical for effective Lean Risk Management because it is both an overview of your risk profile and a tool for managing those risks. Without a risk register, the various risks you identified in the risk inventory exercise may get lost or ignored. With a risk register, however, you have a single consolidated punch list of high-value activities within your organization. You know what is going on with each risk, and you understand how each compares with other threats and opportunities facing the organization.

## Build Your First Risk Register

So how do you create and begin using the risk register? The process is simple.

### *Develop a Risk Task Force*

If you have completed a risk inventory, you likely have identified potential participants in an ad hoc group that can focus on risk within your organization. Now is a good time to formalize that group as a risk task force (RTF). The RTF's duties will not be onerous; it will simply meet periodically to ensure that the risk register is being used and to suggest improvements to the process.

An initial RTF should not be a highly formal affair. It is instead the loose coalition of people in your nonprofit who initially commit to (or are drafted to) pay attention to and test out risk management.

### *Appoint a Risk Reporter*

One person within your organization should be appointed the keeper of the risk register, called the *risk reporter*. This risk reporter may allow other people to edit the risk register, but the risk reporter is ultimately responsible for keeping the risk register current and accurate.

Smaller organizations may be tempted to appoint the executive director or CEO as risk reporter. This book advises, however, that someone besides the executive director serve as risk reporter so that the head of the organization can be in dialogue with at least one other person about this document. (In larger organizations, a chief operating officer, director of risk management or compliance, or even inside legal counsel may be an appropriate risk reporter.)

## Create an Excel or Other Electronic Spreadsheet

You need to create a spreadsheet. The spreadsheet should have seven columns: Priority, Issue, Functional Area, Description, Champion, Next Response, and Check-In Date, in that order. Use Microsoft Excel, Google Sheets, or some similar program that permits substantial functionality with minimal complexity.

## Populate the Spreadsheet

In filling out the spreadsheet, draw directly from the results of the risk inventory exercise and subsequent prioritization exercise described in Chapters 3 and 4. Generally, any risk that received votes should land on the initial risk register, though in most cases a risk register should be limited to no more than 30 or 40 active entries.

- **Priority.** At the end of the prioritization exercise, the executive director or CEO changes the numerical votes from that exercise into a set of priority groupings—say 1 (as highest) to 5 (as lowest). Although you can choose any number of levels, the results of the prioritization exercise tend to shake out naturally into a small set of high-ranking items (the 1s and 2s), a number of middle-range items (3s), and a large number of items that received a few but relatively insignificant number of votes (4s and 5s).
- **Issue.** Provide a brief label for the threat or opportunity. Try to make that label short but descriptive. The idea behind this column is to have a common shorthand reference for the risk within your nonprofit. For example, if the full description of the risk is "Old plumbing in the ceiling of the IT room, posing the possibility of leaks that affect sensitive data," the shorthand label might be "IT water leak threat."
- **Functional Area.** In this column, note the functional area in which this risk arises. (This refers directly back to the risk inventory exercise, in which your team identified threats and opportunities across 11 different functional areas, plus external

risks.) This column is designed to enable your team to readily see where various risks are grouped within your organization.

- **Description.** Here, provide a brief description of the threat or opportunity as you currently understand it. The initial description will come from your risk inventory exercise, modified by any group discussion during that exercise. Over time, the description of the risk will likely change as you gain additional information about the risk. (See "Research" in Chapter 6.)
- **Champion.** In this column, assign a risk champion for the particular risk. The risk champion of a risk is responsible for ensuring that there is action with respect to that threat or opportunity and reporting back with respect to those steps.

Sometimes, a risk champion will be the head of the functional area in which a risk arises. Sometimes, the risk champion will be a subordinate within that function. Occasionally, someone outside the function will be responsible for a risk.

Small organizations may be tempted to list the executive director or CEO as risk champion for many risks. Again, resist this temptation. It is always preferable for someone subordinate to the executive director or CEO to be responsible for championing a risk, because the leader of the organization should be in dialogue with at least one other person on staff. It can't all be on your shoulders.

Sometimes a risk will require involvement from board members. The risk register is an operational document, however, and boards of directors should not be directly involved in operational activities. In cases when a board task force may be involved, assign as risk champion someone on staff who will serve as liaison to the task force. (In very small nonprofits, sometimes there is no staff. In that case, board members will function as risk champions and members of the RTF.)

- **Next Response.** In this column, list the next reportable response, according to the risk champion's plan to address the risk. The next response item will change as the risk champion takes steps to address the risk. For more on the next response, see Chapter 6.

- **Check-In Date.** In this column, the risk reporter lists the date by which the risk champion will report back with respect to this threat or opportunity. Of course, check-in dates will change periodically as the responses themselves change.

The potential benefits of the risk register should be evident. The document provides a brief reference list of the top threats and opportunities facing your nonprofit. Because it is in spreadsheet format, you can sort the document to see when you should expect responses (check-in date), identify who is working on what and whether anyone is overburdened with their risk responsibilities (risk champion), or highlight organizational risk hotspots (functional area).

## FAQs About Your Risk Register

Experience with the risk register typically leads to a series of questions.

### Should I Share the Risk Register with My Entire Staff?

Reasonable minds may differ, but this book recommends that the risk register initially be shared only with the RTF. Later, as risk management becomes more deeply embedded in the organization, you may choose to share the risk register more broadly. You do not want to commit your organization to any risk management approach without first testing the process in a small-scale pilot. It is much easier to control feedback within a small group. Furthermore, adopting a Lean Risk Management process involves a culture shift for some organizations. Keeping the initial register within a smaller group of committed personnel enables you to identify and address potential challenges. Finally, to the extent the risk register contains sensitive information, you may wish to control access to that information.

## Should I Share the Risk Register with My Board?

Board responsibilities with respect to risk management are addressed in Chapter 8. The brief answer is that your first risk register is primarily an operational document that should reside with your staff rather than your board (unless your nonprofit is so small that it functions without staff). You should, however, advise your board that you have created a risk register. Furthermore, as described in Chapter 8, you should inform the board about the top risks identified in that risk register so that the board can weigh in on the most important threats and opportunities facing the organization.

## Should I Share the Risk Register with Anyone Else?

You may wish to share your risk register or risks on the register with the professionals you rely on for advice, including your attorney, your accountants, your insurance brokers, and your banker (if you have a consultative relationship with that person). Those professionals may be able to provide important input about these issues. (Sharing your risks with such outsiders may create confidentiality concerns, so make sure to seek advice before doing so.)

## How Often Should Our Risk Task Force Meet to Review the Risk Register?

The answer will vary with the size and complexity of the organization. Initially, try a monthly or twice-a-month cadence. Later, as the process matures and more employees throughout the organization begin implementing risk management in their daily activities, the RTF may meet every other month or even quarterly (although smaller groups working on particular risks may meet quite regularly).

## What Should We Do on the Check-In Date for a Particular Risk?

A check-in date is a due date for a response. When a check-in date arrives, the risk champion should be held accountable for reporting out the status of that risk, the steps taken to address it, and any modification of the risk description to account for current circumstances.

## How Should Risk Champions Update the Risks for Which They Are Responsible?

Risk champions will update their risks on check-in dates. For interim changes (on fast-moving items or issues where new information becomes available), the risk champion should send an email to the risk reporter describing how the risk register should be changed. Creating an email trail enables both parties to be held accountable for documenting the fact of communication.

## What Should I Do About Threats and Opportunities That Did Not Make It into the Risk Register?

As noted, not all threats and opportunities identified during your risk inventory exercise will make it into the risk register. Competent risk management involves the exercise of reasonable business judgment, which includes deciding to focus on some issues and not others. Still, the potential issues identified in the risk inventory exercise that did not make it into the risk register should not be wholly dismissed.

Instead, create a parking lot document listing the risks that did not make the cut. An easy way to do this is to create a second sheet in the risk register workbook listing those additional risks. At a reasonable time after the initial risk register is created, the RTF should review that parking lot sheet to consider whether any of those risks (or entirely new risks) should be added to the risk register.

*How Else Will We Use the Risk Register?*

As described in Chapter 7, you will use the risk register as a basis for discussion of risks at senior staff meetings and, eventually, meetings with mid-level and frontline personnel. The risk register can serve as a dynamic accountability device throughout the organization, stimulating ongoing discussion of organizational priorities and activities.

You will make further adjustments to this register later, but for now, celebrate! If you have created an initial risk register, you are much further along the path of resilience than almost all your peers. Research suggests that close to 90 percent of nonprofits do not use this basic resilience tool.[1] That means you are already in very select company.

## Insight and Exploration

1. For a downloadable spreadsheet in Microsoft Excel, go to https// riskalts.com/resilienceresources.

2. The columns in a risk register are flexible. Some organizations add a Progress column between Next Response and Check-In Date so that they can record how the risk has been addressed over time. Test and adapt your risk register in response to your nonprofit's experience.

# PART

# III

# Respond

"*There are steps any organization, regardless of its size or sophistication, can take to address or mitigate risks.*"[1]

# 6

## Respond to Your Risks

RUBRICS CAN HELP leaders think through what to do about threats and opportunities. This chapter proposes a framework or rubric for responding to risks.

In general, there are six approaches to dealing with a risk: research, avoidance, mitigation, development (of opportunities), shifting, and monitoring (see Figure 6.1).

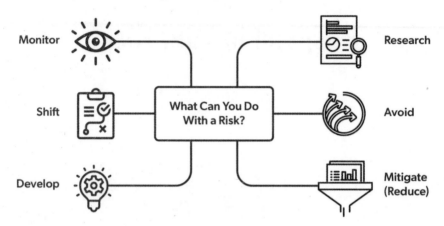

Figure 6.1    What Can You Do to a Risk?

**Research** involves defining and refining the issue that needs response.

You **avoid** a risk by not doing the conduct that might trigger the threat.

You **mitigate** a threat by taking steps to reduce the likelihood of an event happening, reduce the magnitude of the threat if it happens, or increase the amount of time between when you learn the threat is going to create a problem and when that problem fully affects your organization.

Some risks, as discussed, are positive. You do not want to avoid or mitigate opportunities; instead, you want to **develop** them.

If you cannot avoid a risk and mitigation would not bring the risk down to a tolerable level or is not worth the effort, you might consider **shifting** the risk using insurance, contract principles, or partnering with some other organization.

Finally, you may decide to simply **monitor** a risk. If you have done everything you reasonably can to address the risk, you may wish to simply check in on it from time to time, based on some accepted criteria.

Experience shows that these potential responses should be considered in the order presented. Research comes before avoidance, avoidance before mitigation, and so on. In fact, the flow chart shown in Figure 6.2 provides a methodology for

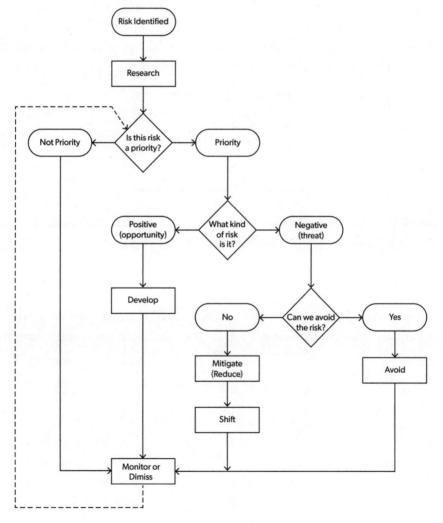

**Figure 6.2   How to Address Risks**

addressing any risk. When a risk is first identified, usually you will perform research to understand its nature. Then you determine its priority. If it is not a priority, you would either monitor or dismiss the risk. If it is a priority, you would consider whether it is a threat or an opportunity. If the risk is an opportunity, you develop it (consistent with its priority and your resources). If it is a threat, you ask whether you can avoid it. If you cannot do so without jeopardizing your mission or core programs, you mitigate it to the extent reasonable, then shift the residual risk to the extent that is appropriate. After treating risks, you monitor them in light of your responses. As circumstances change, you may perform additional cycles of treatment if the risk remains a priority.

*Research*  The first step for most risks, researching a risk involves two separate but related activities: defining and refining.

## *Defining a Risk*

Imagine a colleague came up to you and said, "Here's a gun. We need to kill all the heffenwoofers." You might react with a few questions:

- What is a heffenwoofer?
- Why do we need to kill them?
- Do we need to kill all of them?
- Why use a gun?

Until you have a better idea of what your colleague wants and why, you may not achieve their actual desired outcome.

The example is purposely silly, but imagine this actual heffenwoofer from a nonprofit colleague: "Too many of our remote workers now have side gigs to make extra money that interfere with the performance of their jobs." An increasing number of nonprofit leaders regularly raise this threat. Analytically, one would want to push back on that risk, seeking greater clarity:

- You say "too many." How many? How do you know that? Do you intend to imply that it would be okay for some number of workers to have such additional side jobs?
- You say "remote" workers. Is this an issue only for remote workers? And what do you mean by remote workers—workers who *never* come into an office, or something else?
- You say "side gigs." What do you mean by this term? Do any current policies or procedures speak to what an employee can do with time that is not allocated to your organization?
- You mention "interfere." Describe the circumstances that trigger you to use this word.
- You use the phrase "performance of their jobs." Do the workers in question have written job descriptions? Do they have performance metrics?

Asking questions like these help establish a common understanding of what the challenge is and how it manifests in the workplace.

In medicine, doctors distinguish between the presenting problem and the diagnosis. The presenting problem is the symptom or event that triggers someone to seek professional help from a provider. A patient may come to a doctor complaining of an upset stomach that happens every time she eats spicy food. The doctor will use that presenting problem as one element for evaluation. But the doctor will not stop there. They will ask questions and may perform diagnostic tests and assessments.

In the same way, the first step in addressing a risk is to establish a clearer understanding of what is really at issue. As the first step in researching risk, therefore, use the following questions as a template for conversation:

- **What does this risk mean to you?** This seeks additional descriptive terms.
- **Can you give me concrete examples?** This helps to exemplify with actual factual data.
- **In your experience, how important is this risk relative to other issues we face?** This helps to gauge the relative importance of the risk.
- **In your experience, how does this risk tend to manifest?** This asks for patterns of conduct and experience.
- **Who knows most about this risk inside and outside the organization?** This asks for additional people who might provide relevant facts. It also raises the possibility that external resources may be tapped to create greater understanding and potential solutions.
- **What would solving this risk mean to you?** This asks team members to imagine and describe a future state in which this risk was reduced to a manageable level. That inquiry helps to define a goal and may trigger additional lines of inquiry.

By working through successive discussions using these questions, your team can create a shared understanding of what the issue is and what the organization would look like if the risk were resolved.

When defining a risk, it is critically important to see as clearly as possible. Actually observe the risk in action. If it is part of a process, watch people perform that process. Do not rely merely on reports of what is happening. Consider—but do not rely on—the documentation of a process. As Carlos Venegas notes in his book *Flow in the Office*, "The biggest mistake a team can make is using existing documentation as a proxy for what actually happens in the office."[1] Instead, as Lean practitioners would put it, "stand in the circle": watch the actual performance of the task or tasks that create the risk.[2] Observe the facts and circumstances with as much objectivity as possible.

## Refining a Risk

In addition to defining the risk, your team may wish to also refine the description over time. Refining is a process of getting to the essence of an issue, improving understanding by making small changes and deepening awareness and understanding. Several tools are available to help teams refine risks:

- **5 Whys.** The 5 Whys methodology, originally developed by Sakichi Toyoda for use within the Toyota Motor Company, pushes a team to gain understanding of root causes of a problem by repeatedly asking and answering the question "why?"[3]
- **FMEA.** FMEA stands for Failure Mode and Effects Analysis. FMEA was developed by the US military during the 1940s to help teams conserve precious resources. The exercise challenges team members to identify how things could go wrong and what would happen if they did. Thus, for instance, a team might list each step in a process that is causing concern. For each step the team could ask what could go wrong and what countermeasures should be put in place or triggered when the failure manifests.[4]
- **Premortem.** A premortem exercise engages a team to think about failure.[5] The premortem exercise takes its name from the notion of a postmortem. In a medical setting, doctors will often examine a dead patient to determine the cause of death. A premortem is the hypothetical opposite. Rather than hypothesizing potential failure modes and effects, the premortem

challenges participants to assume that the process has failed, and work backward to brainstorm reasons why. In this way, a team applies prospective hindsight, which can improve outcomes. Premortems and FMEAs serve the same purpose: encourage a team to think about potential hurdles and failures so that they can take effective precautions.

- **Fishbone Diagram.** A Fishbone Diagram (often called a cause and effect diagram or an Ishikawa Diagram, after its creator, Kaoru Ishikawa) provides teams with a visual tool for identifying factors that might cause a threat to materialize.[6]

Refining a risk ordinarily also involves book research, computer research, or data collection. Few truly new challenges arise in human experience. As Nassim Nicholas Taleb observes, "So often it is the mistakes of others that benefit the rest of us—and sadly, not them."[7] Someone has likely faced the same or closely similar circumstances in the past. Why not learn from their experience? Why bloody your own forehead when you can learn from the injuries of others?

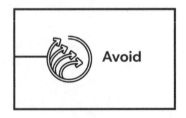

*Avoid* The next approach to addressing a particular risk involves avoiding a risk altogether. How do you avoid a risk? **You do not do the conduct that implicates or triggers the risk.**

That statement might sound trite, but it veils a profound truth. **You can only avoid risks that are entirely within your control.**

Can you avoid an earthquake? Practically speaking, no. The movement of Earth's tectonic plates and their potential consequences to someone on the Earth's surface is beyond your control. You could hypothetically suspend yourself in the air, but there is no way to do that practically or permanently. You could move to an area that is not prone to earthquakes, but that does not actually avoid the possibility of a freak earthquake in your new locale.

Can you avoid someone lying about your organization? Not really. You do not control the words people outside your organization use. As for your employees, you can prohibit conduct and impose consequences for violations, but you cannot impose a foolproof prior restraint on their potential speech.

Can you avoid an investigation by the Internal Revenue Service (IRS)? Not unless you are willing to earn nothing that the IRS might consider income. You can file your taxes and cautiously abide by the rules, but you cannot prevent the IRS from nevertheless making inquiries about your filings. Nor can you avoid such investigation by failing to file: the IRS commits resources to find those who do not abide by filing obligations.

Still, although many risks are unavoidable, some are within your control. You could eliminate a program that triggers the risk, or you could eliminate an activity that triggers the risk.

Take a practical example of eliminating a program. A non-profit provides two programs. One provides aftercare support and educational enrichment for grade school children. The other provides online training to help parents support their children's educational journey. In the child aftercare support and enrichment program, the nonprofit currently picks children up from local schools and transports them to the nonprofit's offices, where program services are provided. The nonprofit realizes that this program creates distinct threats. For example, drivers might drive unsafely and cause accidents or may treat children in an unacceptable manner.

Is this an avoidable risk for the nonprofit? Absolutely. The nonprofit could choose to terminate that program. The threats would vanish. No doubt, other threats may be triggered, including parent anger, loss of funders, and the possibility the organization may have to restate its mission. These additional threats may make avoiding the risk altogether inadvisable. But at least in theory, the risk is avoidable.

What about eliminating an activity that triggers a risk? Consider a different example relating to the same nonprofit. In the online training program for parents, the nonprofit currently uses a standard intake form. That form collects each parent's Social Security number, because historically that was a convenient way to keep track of parents in a database. In looking at that program critically, the executive director recognized that if the organization suffered a data breach, parents' names and Social Security numbers might be compromised.

Is this avoidable? Yes. The nonprofit could modify its intake forms to remove the demand for Social Security numbers.

In short, avoidance may be possible for many threats, but only for those that are within your organization's control.

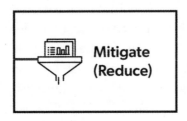

*Mitigate*   As noted, it is often hard to avoid threats entirely. When you cannot or do not want to avoid a risk, mitigation is the next logical alternative.

Mitigation focuses on three characteristics of impact (see Figure 6.3). Mitigation efforts may focus on reducing the likelihood of an adverse event happening. Efforts may focus on reducing the impact of an adverse event if it happens. Or mitigation efforts may focus on creating early warning systems that would give an organization more time in which to deal with an event.

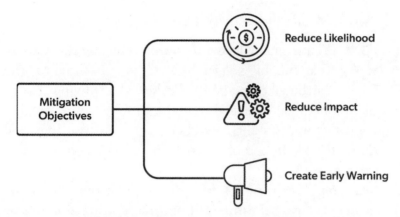

**Figure 6.3 Mitigation Objectives**

Eight different levers can assist an organization in mitigating risks (see Figure 6.4).

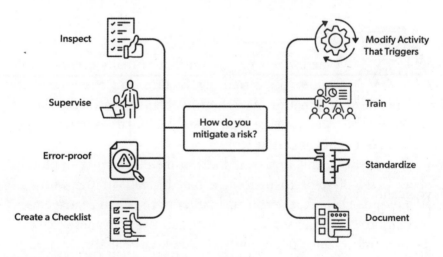

**Figure 6.4 How Do You Mitigate a Risk?**

## Modify the Activity That Triggers the Risk

You might reduce a threat by changing the activity that might trigger the threat. Return to the earthquake example. Rather than living in an earthquake-prone area, one might choose to relocate to a region with greater tectonic stability. By changing where you live, you have reduced the likelihood of suffering the adverse consequences of an earthquake.

In the example of the nonprofit with the aftercare program, the nonprofit may mitigate the threats from transporting children by modifying the program to eliminate transportation. Parents might instead be required to drop children off at the nonprofit's offices. Such a change would eliminate or at least substantially reduce the likelihood of the nonprofit being responsible for accidents or wrongful conduct during the drive.

## Train

One form of mitigation that virtually every organization does is training. By providing team members with practical information about how to perform a particular skill or behavior, the nonprofit reduces the likelihood of intentional, reckless, or negligent conduct.

The best training, however, does not merely instruct employees about a set of steps to perform a job. Instead, in the words of W. Edwards Deming, the spiritual father of the Lean Management revolution, "Training for a job must teach the customer's needs."[8] Team members must understand who their customer is, what they want, and how they want it. Without that information, employees will be mere automatons rather than engaged thought workers who strive for continuous improvement and elimination of waste throughout an organization.

## Standardize

Standardizing—that is, making a process the same each time—serves as an important minimizer of threats. As Robert Pryor notes, "A repeatable process is called for when your aim is to produce the same or very similar outcome from a process, so that the deliverable (a product or service) is the same each time (a widget gets built and shipped, a car is fixed, the patient is treated)."[9] The idea behind standardization is, again in Deming's words, "to accomplish ever greater and greater consistency of performance within the system, so that apparent differences between people continually diminish."[10] Until a process within an organization is standardized, errors will develop because different people are performing the same task differently. Once a process is standardized, an organization can then develop a performance baseline on which to improve.

## Document

Documentation is one of the most effective ways of mitigating risks. If people have clear direction that they can refer to while they perform their tasks, they will make fewer mistakes. However, as Robert Pryor again notes, "Unless your organization is unusual in that it uses a Zen form of communicating information, rules, and culture, it is a safe bet that any process that is not documented is not being followed by everyone, or maybe anyone."[11]

Documentation can take two forms. The first is long-form description of a process, step-by-step. The second is simple visual diagrams that direct activity at the point of engagement. Both serve to mitigate risks.

**Process Descriptions** When most people think of documentation, they think of a manual or set of instructions. These have value, and an organization should reduce its most important processes and the processes that create greatest threats to meaningful step-by-step instructions.

When drafting such instructions, make them no longer than necessary. As author Gino Wickman notes, "If you document 100 percent of the core process, it might take 30 pages. If you document the most important 20 percent, you should need around six pages."[12] Strive for brevity and clarity.

When documenting a process, however, make sure you capture what is actually going on. Karen Martin and Mike Osterling note in their book *Value Stream Mapping* that when describing a process, there are usually at least four versions: "how managers believe it operates, how it's supposed to operate (i.e., the written procedure, if one exists), how it really operates, and how it could operate."[13] As you develop documentation, be sure that it reflects reality.

**Visual Signposting** In addition to providing brief written instructions, an organization mitigates potential risks by creating clear visual cues at the point at which the risky activity occurs.[14] One sees examples of this all the time on a well-run warehouse floor: painted lanes show where trucks are permitted to drive; painted boxes on the floor show where pallets should be placed. The same practices can be imported into an office environment. Online forms can have clear instructional callouts to make sure important information is captured the right way. Posters near activity settings can describe critical safeguards.

## Create Checklists

Documentation and sign-posting can be augmented by creating simple checklists to avoid potential errors and problems. Nonprofits often hesitate to create such checklists, contending that their interactions with beneficiaries are too nuanced and free-flowing to reduce to a set of tick marks. One rejoinder is captured by Atul Gawande in his book, *The Checklist Manifesto*. Gawande is a professor in the

Department of Health Policy and Management at the Harvard School of Public Health and a professor at Harvard Medical School. He notes that checklists—from vital signs to much more complex procedures—save thousands of lives in emergency rooms each day. If hospitals can benefit from checklists, surely most nonprofits can, too.

Gawande notes that checklists ordinarily should not try to be exhaustive. Instead, they should capture the most critical points in a process:

> There are good checklists and bad . . . Bad checklists are vague and imprecise. They are too long; they are hard to use; they are impractical. . . . Good checklists, on the other hand, are precise. They are efficient, to the point, and easy to use even in the most difficult situations. They do not try to spell out everything—a checklist cannot fly a plane. Instead, they provide reminders of only the most critical and important steps—the ones that even the highly skilled professionals using them could miss. Good checklists are, above all, practical.[15]

### Error-Proof

Another way to mitigate risks is to build "error proofing" into the activities at issue. In Japanese, there is a word for this concept—*poka-yoke*, from the Japanese *yokeru*, which means "to avoid," and the word *poka*, which means "inadvertent errors."[16] Again, we see this in workshops and on the factory floor. Carpenters use simple strings to constrain measurements and draw patterns. Machinists use dies and molds to reduce errors that would occur if workers shaped items freehand. We see error proofing at fast food restaurants, where workers put a fountain drink cup under a spigot and press a button that dispenses a precise amount of soda. We see it in website design, where online documents will not accept the submission without all necessary inputs. Nonprofits can similarly create constraints on their processes to ensure that people perform tasks the right way.

*Supervise*

A nonprofit can mitigate risks by ensuring that team members are supervised in the performance of important tasks. Supervision supplements training; training tells people how they should perform their duties, and supervision provides ongoing support, correction, and guidance.

*Inspect*

One final way to mitigate risks is to impose some form of inspection on the process. Nonprofits do this as a matter of routine on grant applications, for example, where someone in authority reviews the finished product before it leaves the organization.

Of course, inspection at the end of a process is not the best possible form of mitigation. As Deming noted, "Inspection to improve quality is too late, ineffective, costly."[17] Following Deming, consider inspection to be a necessary last-chance form of risk mitigation. Still, employees who know that their work may be inspected may take greater care in the performance of their tasks.

*Develop* A key aspect of Lean Risk Management involves developing positive risks—new initiatives or modifications to existing activities to unlock additional value for the nonprofit or its beneficiaries. What follows are steps and considerations that support effective new initiatives.

*Pilot*

Nonprofit resources are too scarce to spend indiscriminately. As Jay Abraham says, "Never test big if you can test small."[18] Or as

Gerald Langley and colleagues note in their book *The Improvement Guide*:

> The idea of testing a change does not seem to come naturally. People tend to want to solve all their problems with one change, and they try to implement the whole change with one plan. Being successful at testing changes requires a very different approach. A test should be designed so that as little time, money, and risk as possible are invested while at the same time almost as much is learned from the test as would be learned from a full-scale implementation of the change.[19]

For any pilot program, six elements will improve the likelihood of success:

1. **Set goals.** Be clear about what you intend and what would constitute success.
2. **Develop metrics.** Identify concrete, measurable criteria to determine how you will measure results.
3. **Create a time line and milestones.** Define at the outset the length of time you are willing and able to commit to the pilot project. Hold yourself accountable. Also, determine stages at which reflection and potential course correction can occur.
4. **Make it real.** Do not set the pilot up artificially for success or failure. To the extent possible, use a representative sample of target beneficiaries so that the results are not skewed from reality.
5. **Gather data.** A pilot team can get so engrossed in performing the new activity that it fails to gather and record data that can determine success or failure.
6. **Capture feedback.** At the conclusion of the project, gather information from those who were involved—both those performing the activity within the nonprofit and those who were the intended beneficiaries. What worked? What did not? If this process were to be improved, what would you suggest? As Langley and colleagues note, "The success of a test lies in what is learned from it, no matter how it turns out."[20]

## Consider the Customer(s)

Many improvement and innovation projects run afoul of a basic consideration: what does the actual customer want? For example, an organization may identify its development process as a worthy target of change. Team members may feel that the development process feel that it is burdensome for the nonprofit, requires too many documents, and does not have a set cadence. All that may be true, but each of those considerations focuses only on the nonprofit. The nonprofit's employees are not the principal customer here. Donors are a meaningful customer in the development process. Donors give money to an organization in exchange for a promise to use that money to achieve certain objectives. As one considers modifications to a nonprofit development process, it would be important to consider the donor as well as the development staff.

In crafting an effective pilot program to capture an opportunity, consider using design thinking concepts. Design thinking, championed by innovators such as Tim Brown, is a structured methodology for considering how customers interact with their environment to address actual customer needs.[21] The design thinking process emphasizes empathy, evolving definitions of a challenge, prototyping potential solutions, and testing. (You can find numerous design thinking book recommendations in the "Sources and Methodology" section at the end of this book.)

## Think in Systems

No change occurs in isolation. Your nonprofit is a system of processes. Your beneficiaries and stakeholders interact among many different systems. A change in one part of the system may often have unexpected consequences in another part of the same system. In considering a pilot program, reflect on the ecosystem in which the initiative exists. Be alert to unintended results. (As with design thinking, numerous book recommendations relating to systems theory are listed in the "Sources and Methodology" section of this book.)

## Perform a Premortem or FMEA

It may seem counterintuitive, but when you create a pilot program, it helps to think about failure. Thus, as when researching a threat, performing a premortem or FMEA is an important part of piloting a change or new initiative. (These tools were mentioned in the "Refining a Risk" section.)

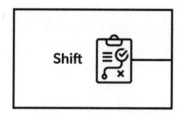

*Shift* Another tested strategy for dealing with risk is to shift the downside concern onto others. Three common approaches dominate the field: insurance, contract, and collaboration. Each of these three approaches have substantial levels of nuance and complexity. They could comprise entirely separate books, and indeed there are some great ones available.[22] As a result, this book merely notes the existence of these possible strategies.

## Consider Insurance

When many people think of risk management, they think of insurance. As noted in Chapter 1, insurance permits an insured to shift a potential threat onto some other party. If the event occurs, the other party will reimburse for some or all the covered loss.

It is remarkable the variety of insurance coverage available, but with that breadth comes substantial complexity. This book is not about insurance, and insurance is technical and detailed. When considering insurance, reach out to an insurance agent who can guide you through the issues. When you do, be careful to explain all the relevant facts to the agent; insurance coverage depends on candor and completeness.

## Consider a Contract

Loosely, a contract is an agreement between two or more parties that allocates rights and responsibilities between them. Behind those words lies another vast mountain of complexity, but the basic concept of a contract has direct implications for risk management. Nonprofits order their business affairs by contract all the time. They have contracts with vendors, staff members, and end users of their goods and services. Those contractual arrangements may often be modified to shift threats from one party to another.

Just as discussion of insurance suggests the need for an experienced broker, using contracts to manage risks requires the advice of an attorney.

## Consider Collaboration

Together collaborators can do things that they could only dream of separately. By working with a partner organization, you can capture upside potential while sharing downside risks. Indeed, one of the best exercises a nonprofit can perform involves identifying and evaluating its ecosystem.[23] By identifying resource providers, competitors, allies, beneficiaries, opponents, and bystanders, the nonprofit can build a strategy for meaningful, productive collaboration. Although collaboration is outside the scope of this book, tremendous value can be achieved by creating networks of practice and accountability.

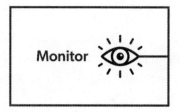

*Monitor* For many risks, the appropriate response is simply to monitor them. Perhaps you have determined that they are not a current priority. Perhaps you have mitigated them as much as you reasonably can.

In deciding to monitor a risk, consider whether you can identify an event or threshold of incidence that would trigger enhanced scrutiny.

## Insight and Exploration

1. The various steps you take to address a risk—your risk treatments—will vary over time. Although the diagram at the beginning of this chapter shows a normal flow, a risk champion may create subloops that cycle back to previous treatments. This is especially true with research. As you begin to address a risk, you will identify issues that you do not understand or that someone else may have addressed in the past.

2. Notwithstanding the diagram at the beginning of this chapter, some risks will be simple binary identify it/solve it issues. If something really is simple, just do it.

# PART

# IV

# Assess and Improve

*"What an organization needs is not just good people; it needs people that are improving with education."* [1]

# 7

---

# Develop a Risk Management Cycle

Once you have created your risk register, you want to use it. This chapter provides guidance about how to make the most out of this important tool, which forms the basis of your risk management cycle (see Figure 7.1).

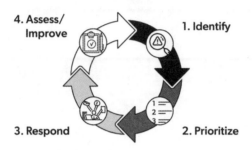

Figure 7.1    Risk Management Cycle

## Review Your Risk Register Regularly

Similar to any other tool, the risk register will help only if you use it. With your first risk register, pull the document out at least once every two weeks. Informally check in with each of your risk champions to see how they are doing on the risks for which they are responsible.

## Develop a Cadence for Risk Management Discussions

As noted throughout this book, resilience is not an event but rather a process. Your team should discuss how often it should review the risks facing the organization.

A nonprofit just beginning to use Lean Risk Management should meet about risks at least once or twice a month. Some nonprofits will set a separate meeting to focus on risk management. Others will use an agenda item in a standing meeting either once or twice a month.

Whatever cadence you decide, realize that you will change and adjust over time. After three months, you may find that you can meet less regularly (once a month or even once a quarter). Alternatively, you might find that you need to meet more regularly or segregate time for specific discussions of risk register items.

## Use the Risk Register as the Basis for Meetings About Risk Management

Use your risk register as the grounding document that helps your team focus its discussions about risk. You want risk discussions to be meaningful and productive; having a document that shows the status of each priority risk gives you a unifying concept for risk management meetings.

## Make a Copy of the Risk Register at Least Once a Month

At the close of each month, instruct your risk reporter to make a new version of the register and/or a PDF of the existing register. You do this because you want to capture progress (or lack of progress) over time. Making a copy as part of your end of month tasks enables your team to look back months later to see where and when progress was made.

In addition to this monthly copy, consider making a new version of your risk register whenever there is a significant development with respect to one of your risks. Sometimes events move more rapidly than a monthly record would capture; if that is the case, make interim copies.

## Use "No-Vote" Risks as the Basis for Functional Work Sessions

Recall that some of the risks identified in your risk inventory did not get any votes during risk prioritization. That does not mean those potential risks go away. Instead, as mentioned, you capture those additional risks on a separate "parking lot" page of your risk register workbook.

That separate page can be the important basis for additional team discussions. Employees who focus on a particular functional area could review the unranked risks in that functional area to have a discussion of whether any should be promoted to the front page. Employees may find that discussion of these unranked risks is critical to the nonprofit's performance. For instance, a risk may languish on the unranked page simply because somebody was inarticulate in describing the risk during the inventory. A function-specific meeting may tease out the true meaning of risks that were insufficiently clear during inventory and prioritization.

## Add New Risks as They Arise

In your periodic meetings about risk management, capture new risks as people identify them. When doing so, add the risk to the bottom of your register, without priority, and afterwards reflect where the risk should fit among existing priorities. Use the rubric from Chapter 4 as the basis for your initial prioritization. Once you determine the risk's priority, redirect it to the proper place in the punch list. (If you are using an electronic spreadsheet to keep your risk register, as advised, redirecting a risk to its proper place in the register is a simple matter of using the sort function on the Priority column.)

## Reprioritize Existing Risks as Circumstances Change

Circumstances will inevitably change at your nonprofit. You might find on further exploration that a risk was mistakenly prioritized. Once investigated, you might find that the risk can be taken off the register altogether. A risk might also shift in priority as you take steps to treat it, as discussed in Chapter 6. Or circumstances may change so that a risk that was relatively low priority becomes a much higher priority item.

## Hold Champions Accountable

One reason why we perform risk management as a process is that people will become distracted over time. Your team members will have good intentions, but sometimes they will fail to follow through. Using the risk register and periodic risk management meetings, you can hold team members accountable for progress and explanations.

When doing this, keep in mind that some of your risk champions may not have the authority to implement necessary changes on their own. Reinforce with all risk champions that they need to come to senior leadership if they need additional support.

## Add Additional Perspectives

As you begin to institutionalize risk management, you can broaden the number of people providing inputs into your risk process. If you followed recommendations in prior chapters, your initial risk inventory and prioritization involved only a small group within your nonprofit. You can expand this input in many different directions.

First, as covered in greater detail in the next chapter, it will become important to seek input from your board of directors about the top risks on the risk register and other risks they feel may need to be added.

Second, over time you can (and should) broaden the number of staff members who provide input into the risk management process. Organizations can do this in many ways. Some will share the risk register (or some portion to it), with additional staff members to get their review and input. This method has the benefit of complete transparency. However, senior leadership may not want to share all the risks with everyone in the nonprofit. Some risks may be sensitive, and others may be insufficiently or inaccurately described in their current state. There is no reason to get all your employees worried about a risk that may be illusory.

An alternative method would be to provide basic awareness training for additional employees over time, and then have those additional employees perform their own risk inventory. That inventory might be constrained to the functional areas in which they operate, or you may choose to have them go through an inventory as broad as the one described in Chapter 3.

Another method that has achieved success with many nonprofits is to have functional leaders hold input sessions with their teams. Those functional leaders then provide updated input to the risk reporter so that new risks are fed into the process.

Whenever you begin to add additional staff perspectives, take care to manage expectations. Staff members should be informed that their input is valued, but they should not expect that every issue they raise will be addressed or solved. Limited resources, different or higher priorities, or other issues might prevent your nonprofit from addressing a staff member's pet peeve. That's not a failure of the process; instead, that's the process working as it should. Risk management, after all, is all about taking the next reasonable step considering the circumstances facing the organization. Such choices always involve trade-offs.

In addition to employees, over time you may wish to solicit ideas about threats and opportunities from those whom your nonprofit services. Your customers, your beneficiaries, may have profound insights about issues affecting your nonprofit. Some insights might involve the nature of the services you provide or how you provide them; others might involve community or contextual issues that have escaped your attention. As with employees, you want to emphasize that your nonprofit cannot implement every recommendation or fix every criticism.

You might broaden input even further. As your risk management process improves, you might seek input from other stakeholders, including peer organizations, government organizations, or funders.

In adding perspectives, take things incrementally. Do not open the floodgates. Instead, test a particular new input for a period before implementing it more broadly.

## Name, Claim, Record, and Celebrate Value

To create momentum and avoid burnout, recognize progress. Positive reinforcement is critically important to long-term success.

To do this, name, claim, record, and celebrate (NCRC) each time you address a risk. Add a third page to your risk register workbook. Here, capture small and large successes along the way, listing the date, the participant(s) in the success, and the nature of the success. Be on the alert for ways in which your risk inventory, risk register, and risk cycle have helped you gain clarity, peace of mind, and value. For example:

- Did your risk inventory foster discussions about important threats and opportunities? Name, claim, record, and celebrate it. Be specific about what issues you were able to discuss that the team had not discussed recently.
- Were you able to clarify any potential risks that different people defined in different ways? NCRC.
- Were you able to determine that any identified risks were, on reflection, not that worrisome? NCRC.
- Did your risk prioritization that created your risk register enable you to have any fruitful discussions about your non-profit's most important issues? NCRC.
- Were you able to research or redefine any risks? NCRC.
- Were you able to avoid any risks? NCRC.
- Were you able to reduce (mitigate) any threats or develop (exploit) any opportunities? NCRC.
- Did you shift any risks using insurance, contract, or collaboration? NCRC.
- Did you meet to talk about risks at all since the last time you reflected on your process? NCRC.
- As a result of beginning to speak more regularly about risks, have you observed any positive changes in team culture? NCRC.

## Emphasize WIIFT with Your Team

While your team members are no doubt magnanimous and unselfish, never ignore human nature. Always emphasize what's in it for them (WIIFT).

Here are some benefits from nonprofit risk management you might highlight in staff discussions:

- Team members gain increased opportunities to fix policies, procedures, programs, and physical dangers that threaten or annoy them.
- Team members get to participate in safeguarding and improving their own safety and health.
- Team members get increased awareness of important issues within the organization that are outside of their traditional swim lanes.
- Team members have opportunities to identify better ways to serve the nonprofit's clientele.
- Team members get greater chances to work on mission-critical threats and opportunities to increase personal and professional development and shine.
- Team members get increased input into how resources are allocated.
- By increasing organizational resilience and sustainability, team members increase their own job protection.

## Develop Support Networks

Finally, do not try to do all this work on your own.

Internally, have at least two people working on any given risk. That way, team members are in dialogue, rather than feeling overwhelmed.

Throughout the organization, institutionalize periodic meetings to reinforce the common cause and share best practices.

The support network, however, should not end at the boundaries of your nonprofit organization. Look outside, too. Find online groups of like-minded nonprofits (like the one Risk Alternatives sponsors called Nonprofits Build Strength Together [BeST]) who can hold you and each other accountable. It helps to have accountability partners and fellow travelers along the same Lean Risk Management path.

## Insight and Exploration

1. For a downloadable checklist of how to develop your risk management cycle, as well as NCRC and WIIFT checklists, go to https//riskalts.com/resilienceresources.

2. You can find a link to BeST on the resilience resources link mentioned above. In addition, consider groups such as the Nonprofit Risk Management Center and Joan Garry's Nonprofit Leadership Lab.

3. As you implement a risk cycle, consider using the questions in Appendix 2 to stimulate discussions within various functional areas of your nonprofit about additional issues that might populate your risk register.

# 8

## Work with Risks at the Board Level

As DEMONSTRATED so far in this book, most of the work of Lean Risk Management for nonprofits happens at the staff level. The board of directors, however, plays a limited but critical role in the risk management process. This chapter describes your board's role.

Thematically, the board's role in nonprofit risk management is largely evaluative, not operational. Except in very small nonprofits that operate without a staff, a board largely sets direction and enables staff to perform its tasks. This concept was captured effectively by Frederick Fungston and Stephen Wagner in their book *Surviving and Thriving in Uncertainty* by the epigram, "Nose in, hands off."[1] The board should ask probing questions. It should participate in the risk management process within established bounds. But it should avoid operational decision-making or second-guessing.

Briefly, the board's role includes three key functions:

- Ensure that staff is performing its critical risk management activities.
- Weigh in on the most important risks facing the organization.
- Set the tone at the top of the organization.

## The Board Should Ensure That Staff Is Performing Its Critical Risk Management Work

The board's first role is to make sure that staff members are performing risk management. The board should periodically ask some or all the following questions:

- Has the staff adopted a formal risk management process?
- Has the staff adopted a regular cadence for implementing a risk cycle?
- Has the risk management cycle led to any changes in the nonprofit's risk register?

- What issues or challenges have staff members faced in performing the risk management function, and what has been done to address those issues?
- What successes or victories have staff achieved because of its risk management work?
- What improvements or modifications to the risk management process are being considered, and why?

## The Board Should Weigh In on the Most Important Risks Facing the Organization

The second role of a board concerning risk management is to weigh in on the most important risks facing the organization. Here, the board provides two different perspectives: one involves reflection and evaluation, and the other involves what may be called generation.

### Reflection and Evaluation

To provide reflection and evaluation, a board should periodically request and receive a list of the top risks facing the organization. An executive director could fulfill this request by providing the top three to five items on the risk register. The board can reflect on those items and discuss their relative priority and possible countermeasures.

In performing this reflection/evaluation function, the board should keep in mind that staff may have considerably greater awareness of functional risks facing the nonprofit. Staff live and breathe these issues every day. A board should probe staff priorities and countermeasures and should discuss whether board members are aware of resources staff can use to address important risks. Ultimately, it is within board authority to overrule staff on risks that implicate strategic outcomes. Boards should exercise that authority to overrule, however, with humility and circumspection. Most volunteer board members will not be in position to credibly second-guess the studied reflection and prioritization of staff members. If a board finds itself fundamentally out of step with its staff, the response is not to micromanage. Instead, the board should work to address board/staff disfunctions.

However, executive directors should encourage reflection, inquiry, and challenge from the board. Board members help staff members avoid tunnel vision. They provide a check on unfettered staff activity.

A properly functioning board will therefore serve as a thought partner with an executive director and staff.

## Generation

In addition to reflecting and evaluating top risks identified by staff, a nonprofit board also provides independent and original insight into additional potential threats and opportunities. Thus, when fulfilling its risk management obligations, a highly functioning board will spend time discussing potential issues that were **not** generated by the staff. Because of their diverse backgrounds and independent endeavors, board members may see problems that have escaped staff attention. They may also be aware of potential new initiatives that might capture value for the nonprofit, as well as new ways to perform existing tasks to improve efficiency and effectiveness.

## The Board Should Set the Tone at the Top of the Organization

Finally, a board should set the tone at the top, emphasizing that risk management, compliance, and sound governance are priorities for the nonprofit. A board leads, in part, by example. By emphasizing that risk management, compliance, and governance are important, a board reinforces and models these concepts for staff members.

## *Adopt a Risk Management Policy—When the Nonprofit Is Ready*

It might seem curious that adopting a risk management policy comes near the end of a work about resilience and nonprofit risk management rather than the beginning. There is a sound basis for this approach. Risk management should be adopted incrementally. Different organizations will respond differently to risk management tools as they are tested and adopted. As a result, a board cannot know what the nonprofit's risk management policy should ultimately look like at the beginning of a risk management journey.

The early testing and assessment of risk management practice is performed by staff, as discussed throughout this book. After a nonprofit has performed an initial inventory, after it has prioritized those risks into a risk register, after it has completed enough risk management cycles, the board will have data on which a sound policy may be adopted.

Appendix 3 provides templates for board risk management policies. These are not exhaustive and should be tailored to a nonprofit's particular circumstances.

---

**What About Risk Tolerance and Risk Appetite?**
Some board members will no doubt be aware that sophisticated organizations will often adopt board policies addressing risk tolerance and risk appetite. Briefly, risk tolerance is an attempt to set parameters on how much risk an organization *can* shoulder if things go wrong. Analogously, risk appetite is an articulation of how much risk an organization *wants* to shoulder. In our experience, most nonprofits do not have the research resources and modeling capacity to undertake sophisticated risk tolerance and risk appetite exercises. As a result, those topics are outside the scope of this book.

## Before a Policy Is Adopted, Focus on FRaMEs

If your board wants to help staff as that team is beginning to test risk management principles, board members could inquire about whether the nonprofit has adopted certain background policies and processes that implicate and improve risk management. Those items, as mentioned previously, may be called *fundamental risk management elements*, or FRaMEs. They include items such as insurance, whistleblower policies, conflict-of-interest policies, and the like. A board task force could readily use a checklist of FRaMEs to reflect on basic items the staff could work on over time to improve the overall risk profile of the organization. Appendix 4 provides a list of FRaMEs that your board or staff can use.

## Ensure the Nonprofit Has an Effective Compliance Function

Although this book focuses on risk management, setting the tone at the top involves issues beyond risk management. An effective board should secure reasonable assurance that staff has a solid compliance function in place. The nature and rigor of that function will vary depending on the nonprofit's activities, but Appendix 5 provides a checklist of compliance areas.

## Ensure the Board Follows Its Own Rules and Seeks to Improve

A board sets the tone at the top in one final critical way: abiding by its own rules of conduct and seeking to improve over time.

It is surprising and disturbing how often nonprofit boards do not abide by their own bylaws. It's unfortunate but true that many nonprofit board members have not looked at the organization's bylaws or articles of incorporation since joining the board. Informality about board performance will inevitably seep down into operational areas of the nonprofit. Board members cannot expect staff to abide by the rules if board members themselves flout the rules.

Similarly, a highly effective board seeks to improve over time. It self-consciously evaluates the talents and commitment of existing board members. It seeks new board members who will fill important gaps in knowledge or experience. It looks for and engages in opportunities for training.

In short, your board sets the tone at the top in part by modeling the conduct it expects from its team.

## Insight and Exploration

1. Numerous sources provide information and prescriptions for how to build an effective board of directors. Particularly valuable are websites like BoardSource (boardsource.org) and its publication, *The Nonprofit Board Answer Book*.[2]

2. As noted, in very small nonprofits that do not have a separate staff, board members will function as staff when performing risk management. As a result, the first and second board risk management functions (ensuring performance and weighing in on risks) will occur naturally as part of the risk management process. The third board risk management function, however, should never get lost even in the smallest nonprofit. Boards must set the tone at the top by abiding by their own rules, even where there is no staff. Boards perform a stewardship function for stakeholders, and informality at the board level threatens effective stewardship.

# 9

## Implement Lean Risk Management Incrementally

You would not try to swim from Alcatraz to the city shore at Fisherman's Wharf in San Francisco Bay without first learning to swim and putting in plenty of practice. The same goes for risk management. As with any other long-term effort, you need to take learning about and institutionalizing risk management in your nonprofit one step at a time. The pace of change for your organization depends on your nonprofit's leadership, culture, and financial situation.

This chapter provides an implementation strategy that may differ from other advice you have seen about adopting risk management because this book advocates taking a Lean approach to risk management. This approach focuses on maximizing value while minimizing waste and expenditures.

For those who have read this book from the beginning, the elements of strategy, in summary form, will be familiar because they track the forgoing chapters. This chapter sets out the time line separately so that you can easily share it with your team and stakeholders.

## Dip a Toe in the Water

At the outset of a Lean Risk Management journey, you want to plot a path, gather some initial resources, and take first steps toward implementation. Incrementalism is key.

### 1. Develop a Time Line

Depending on your efforts and the resources you commit, you can expect to develop a functional Lean Risk Management process within about 18 to 24 months.

Of course, you will gain benefits along the way. Some of the early steps of risk management—including your initial risk inventory—yield powerful insights and identify low-hanging fruit, including threats that can be addressed before they ripen into crises and opportunities for changes that yield significant returns.

116

Still, you cannot expect changes overnight. Thus, adopt a time line and lay out tasks to create a tentative schedule. Here is a suggested approach:

**By month 1:** Complete a tentative project time line and allocate minor initial resources.

**By month 2:** Complete a risk inventory.

**By month 3:** Complete an initial risk register.

**By month 4:** Pilot a risk cycle among senior personnel.

**PAUSE** and consider whether you want to proceed. If so,

**By month 6:** Begin institutionalization tasks: identifying stakeholders, seeking sponsors within senior leadership, developing a shared vision, setting goals, and adopting a full budget.

**By month 15:** Complete training of board of directors.

**By month 18:** Complete training of mid-level personnel.

**By month 24:** Complete training of line personnel.

**After month 24:** Perform risk cycles and improve your approach over time.

## 2. Allocate Initial Resources

Initial risk management work is **not** expensive. Using this book, you can do it on your own. Even if you reach out for external support, the initial investment should not cost more than a few thousand dollars for a small nonprofit. When compared to the potentially devastating cost of an unforced error such as those mentioned in Chapter 1, the investment is minimal.

## 3. Perform a Risk Inventory

Adopting a risk management process should be incremental and exploratory. Fortunately, a risk inventory does not require significant budget commitments. It is a toe-in-the-water activity, when a small team within your nonprofit brainstorms (first separately, then together) about threats and opportunities throughout your organization. A risk inventory, therefore, should precede full commitment to adopting Lean Risk Management.

## 4. Develop a Risk Register

Following close on the completion of an initial risk inventory, the organization should develop its first risk register. This involves prioritizing the risks identified in the inventory into the most important threats and opportunities facing the organization, then assigning those risks to risk champions for specific follow-up and shepherding those risks. The assigned champion does not have to do all the work on an assigned risk. They just need to be the point person for action.

## 5. Test a Risk Management Cycle Among Senior Staff

After performing a risk inventory and developing an initial risk register, a nonprofit should test a regular risk management cycle among senior staff. This means raising the risk register as a regular agenda item at senior staff meetings, updating the register to reflect changes as priorities shift when the organization addresses risks, and adding threats and opportunities as those arise in the ordinary course of business.

This milestone is important for many reasons. You need to regularize the notion of risk management within senior staff. You also want to reinforce a common vocabulary among your leadership. Finally, you might need to make some course corrections to your standard operating procedures to account for a regular cadence of risk management.

After completing the first five steps in your time line, take a pause. Assess whether the efforts thus far have been worth it. Consider the following questions:

- Did you experience at least one ah-ha moment during the risk inventory, risk register, and pilot risk cycle? That is, did you uncover any high-value risks, learn something new about the organization, or learn about the way team members perceive risks or interact as a team?
- Have your initial efforts raised any problems that would prevent you from moving forward with risk management?
- Do you need outside assistance to get the full value out of your risk management efforts?
- What learning can you harvest from the first five steps in this time line to make your future efforts more effective?

## Take the Plunge

If you decide to proceed, it is now time to lay a firm foundation for future growth. This is where you actually take the plunge into the deeper water of sustained effort. Adopting risk management involves change management, too. As risk awareness and risk agility begin to affect your culture, vested interests may resist change. As a result, you will need to accomplish basic change management tasks along the path to institutionalizing Lean Risk Management.

Although some might suggest that you perform these tasks when you are just starting out, this book advises taking these steps **after** you have already performed an initial inventory, created an initial risk register, and created a norm of risk management discussion among your senior staff. That way, you will have already gained some of the benefits of risk management awareness, and you will be able to approach the tasks of change management with a greater awareness of the interests and attitudes at stake. So let us look at those change management efforts next.

## 6. *Identify Stakeholders and Their Interests*

It is critical to identify those who have a stake in the implementation and success of a risk management process. Your board, senior staff, line personnel, end users of your services, and donors all have potentially distinct stakes.

**The Board of Directors** As you have learned, risk management is ultimately a governance function: your board of directors is responsible for ensuring that a nonprofit has a functional risk management program. Board members also have important practical stakes in risk management. Board members may serve on nonprofit boards for a variety of reasons, but at the bottom, they are performing a free service because they believe in the mission of the organization. They do not want to be embarrassed or disappointed by risks that affect the organization. They do not want to be held accountable for alleged breaches of their fiduciary duties because of preventable managerial or governance failures. In short, board members benefit from the cover and protection provided by risk management.

Counterbalancing these incentives to adopt risk management, however, is the possibility that some of your board may hesitate to adopt risk management because they perceive it as diverting funds from ultimate end users of the nonprofit's services. Other board members may be unfamiliar with the concepts of risk management— especially the modern concept that risk management should be focused not only on downside risks (threats) but also upside risks (opportunities).

Thus, your board may be a natural ally in adopting risk management, but one cannot presume that every board member will immediately be on board with the concept.

**Senior Staff** Senior staff may have strong incentives to adopt risk management practices. Effective Lean Risk Management can streamline operations and allow senior staff to extend their vision into the everyday activities of the organization. An effective risk management process can provide a window into line operations and serve as a self-sustaining early warning system.

Still, senior staff may be hesitant to adopt risk management. They may worry that a risk management process will highlight their own mismanagement or poor choices. They may also be hesitant to open their functional area to comment and potential criticism from other senior staff members. Finally, they may feel that risk management activities distract them and their direct reports from performing the functional tasks for which they are responsible (and on which their compensation may depend).

**Frontline Personnel** Personnel at the front lines of the nonprofit's operations may have mixed feelings about adopting risk management. To the extent risk management is perceived as adding additional tasks, they may resist. If risk management identifies mistakes and poor performance, they may feel uncomfortable. If they perceive that the culture will not permit them to voice potential concerns, they may hesitate to participate.

However, a risk management process can profoundly energize and empower frontline personnel to take a more active role in their organization. Risk management can provide a channel for constructively voicing frustrations about inefficient and ineffective processes. It can also provide a forum for identifying and exploring new initiatives that could materially improve working conditions and effectiveness within the organization.

**End Users of Nonprofit Goods or Services** The users of your nonprofit's goods and services—your nonprofit's customers—have a direct stake in your risk management process. One core objective of a risk management process is to make an organization a safer, more effective, more sustainable provider of goods and services. Ultimately, current and future recipients of your services are the beneficiaries of those risk management activities.

However, a nonprofit's customers may react negatively to what they perceive as red tape or unnecessary guardrails. As a result, risk management must be approached from the customer's perspective, and changes to address risks should be clearly explained when necessary.

**Donors** Your funders also have an important stake in your risk management work. Ultimately, funders want to see you achieve your objectives. Risk management reduces the chance of unintended consequences arising from risks. It enables you to respond to uncertainty with greater agility. That increases the likelihood that funding will achieve mission-critical objectives.

Still, some funders may worry about an organization devoting funds to overhead and infrastructure instead of end user services. Implementing risk management deliberately and incrementally can address those concerns.

## 7. Seek Senior Leadership Sponsorship

A risk management program needs internal champions to succeed. By now, you will have already tested risk management among senior staff. It is time to decide who will champion ongoing risk management efforts within your organization.

The obvious candidate for risk management leadership is the executive director or CEO. An effective risk management program simply will not succeed if the executive director/CEO does not at least accept it. But beyond merely tolerating risk management, if the executive director fails to make risk management a priority, any risk management function will be stunted. An executive director or CEO can emphasize the priority of risk management by raising the issue with senior leadership, raising the issue with frontline staff, raising the issue with the board of directors, demonstrating an awareness of risk management vocabulary and best practices, and allocating sufficient budgetary resources to risk management. By taking an active role in championing risk management, an executive director or CEO can dramatically improve the likelihood that a risk management process will bear fruit over time.

If the executive director or CEO cannot directly lead the push for risk management, they can delegate this effort to someone else on the senior staff, such as a CFO or director of programs. In that case, the chief executive should make a point of endorsing and supporting the risk management process vocally and consistently.

A risk management process also will not achieve its objectives unless the board of directors supports the effort. This does not mean that the board ordinarily leads in the early stages of risk management adoption. To the contrary, as described in Chapter 8, staff may (and ordinarily should) precede the board in this process. Still, after staff has performed the initial toe-in-the-water tasks, the board should be apprised of the effort so that they can weigh in on this initiative relative to other organizational priorities and emphasize its importance.

## 8. Develop and Foster a Shared Vision

A nonprofit also needs to adopt a shared vision of why the organization is embarking on a risk management initiative. Articulating a shared vision is the critical groundwork for effective risk management. A shared vision can overcome objections. A common understanding of what is at stake can energize teams to perform tasks they would otherwise hesitate to perform. A shared vision can also provide comfort and direction when a project gets bogged down. When the path gets tough, it is important to keep in mind why the destination is important.

Your shared vision for risk management may include some or all the following rationales:

- Meeting recognized best practice standards, including those addressing risk management and process improvement
- Bolstering the strategic planning function by creating a foundation of awareness about the organization's actual capacities and challenges
- Providing measurable increases in safety for personnel and operational resilience for the organization
- Reducing insurance costs
- Demonstrating commitment to risk management to various stakeholders, including those previously identified
- Increasing the visibility of threats and opportunities throughout the organization and the treatments for approaching them
- Developing a process that leads to measurable performance improvement year over year
- Fostering a culture of learning, freedom to express concerns, and willingness to admit errors

## 9. Set Goals

It is not enough to say, "we want to adopt a risk management process." Without concrete goals, it will be impossible to determine whether or when you achieve that outcome.

Assuming you follow the described time line, effective goals from this point may include some or all the following:

- Complete orientation and training of senior staff.
- Complete orientation and training of the board of directors.
- Complete training of line personnel.
- Codify your risk management process in a simple procedure.
- Complete __ straight months of reviewing the risk register at least monthly during one or more senior staff meetings.
- Identify at least __ number of new threats because of regular risk management meetings.
- Identify at least __ number of new opportunities because of regular risk management meetings.
- Increase self-reported staff awareness of risk management, vocabulary, and responsibilities by __ percent.
- Reduce insurance costs by __ percent.

## 10. Develop a Full Budget

Your risk management work will require both time and money. Whether or not you engage an outside consultant to assist you in the process, paying attention to risk management issues will require some staff effort. If you are like most nonprofits, you currently do not have substantial unencumbered personnel available to focus on risk management, but a strong risk management culture and process can be developed in stages, using existing staff in most cases. In a large or very large nonprofit, staffing a Lean Risk Management effort could range from much less than a full-time job to full-time jobs for multiple staff members. In a smaller nonprofit, risk management might be assigned to an existing senior leader.

You can expect your risk management efforts to pay off with reduced time and effort to certain tasks over time, but you cannot expect that payoff to be immediate. You will need to allocate additional resources. Some potential expenditures may include staff time and attention (including potential hires or reallocation of responsibilities), hosting additional training and orientation for new personnel, and creation of key risk management documents, such as a risk management procedure or manual.

Do not skimp. Investments in Lean Risk Management are far less than the cost of even a single public misstep. In this era of instantaneous communication and permanent electronic records, an error can cascade into a crisis overnight. Even if risk management does not prevent crises, the existence of an effective program can provide staff and board of directors with comfort that they are doing their best to steward the organization. Accordingly, when allocating resources toward risk management, you should consider it a bedrock expenditure for the organization.

## Learn to Swim

Having devoted effort to preparing your nonprofit for a shift to greater attention to risk management, you may now proceed with the final steps in your time line.

## 11. Train the Board

As noted previously, this book advises waiting to train your board about risk management until after the organization has performed its initial risk inventory, developed its risk register, and regularized a risk management cycle within senior management. At that point, the board can be trained on its critical but limited function in risk management. This training, too, should not be costly.

## 12. Train Mid-level Personnel

After senior personnel have regularized the risk management cycle within their senior staff meetings, mid-level personnel should be brought into the process. They should learn how to manage up with respect to their supervisors, raising risks and providing updates about progress and challenges.

They should also learn how to manage down to their direct reports, identifying challenges rather than covering them up and encouraging line personnel to provide suggestions for continuous improvement throughout the organization.

## 13. Train Frontline Personnel

Finally, the organization should train frontline personnel about their risk management responsibilities. These may include the following:

- **Act like owners.** Risk management asks frontline personnel to think about how their job is performed **while they perform that job.** Workers should think about how they interact with others to achieve results, and how those interactions might be improved.
- **See something, say something.** Risk management requires frontline personnel to act as the eyes and ears of senior management by identifying threats and opportunities they see in their everyday activities.
- **Abide by policies and processes, but also suggest improvements.** Lean Risk Management emphasizes that an organization must adopt clear policies and procedures to define how workers perform tasks. Clear policies and procedures may prohibit activities that pose a significant risk to the organization, or they may channel activities away from threats. Frontline personnel need to be made aware of the **why** behind rules so that they will more willingly follow instructions. Understanding the why, they may explore how the purpose behind the procedure can be more

effectively achieved. Frontline personnel, therefore, should be trained and empowered to suggest changes in policies and procedures.

■ **Admit mistakes and worries.** Frontline personnel must also learn to be willing to admit mistakes. They need to be encouraged to speak up about their concerns. They should be rewarded for being open and honest about their observations. Ultimately, by training frontline personnel to be vulnerable in this sense, the organization achieves greater strength and resiliency.

## Do Your Laps

Lean Risk Management is ultimately not a destination but a proceeding. As you spread risk awareness throughout your organization, reflect on progress along the way. Some questions for reflection might include the following:

■ When should you go back and perform another thorough risk inventory, this time with more participants?

■ Should you perform separate risk inventories in different departments or functional areas and consolidate them?

■ Are certain functions in the nonprofit more resistant to risk management? If so, is this a function of personality, rules, culture, or something else?

■ How can you continuously improve the process of risk management over time?

Take your time in adopting Lean Risk Management. Be deliberate, and at each stage, pause to see what is working well and what needs improvement.

However long you take, though, be sure to follow through. Your nonprofit's long-term resilience depends on risk management.

## Insight and Exploration

1. A downloadable timetable consistent with this chapter can be found on https//riskalts.com/resilienceresources.

# Conclusion

YOU HAVE COME a very long way in a short time. You have learned that nonprofits need risk management more than other organizations. You have learned the basic vocabulary—*risk*, *threats*, *opportunities*, *risk management*, and *Lean Risk Management*. You have discovered a simple tool—the risk inventory—for identifying threats and opportunities throughout your nonprofit and beyond. You have learned how to prioritize your risks and use your risk register to track progress and hold your team accountable. And you have learned how you can assess and improve your resilience, creating a risk cycle and spreading responsibility, accountability, and risk awareness throughout your nonprofit.

More broadly, nonprofits are asked to accept tremendous responsibilities in our communities. In a just society, we must care for those who are unfortunate. We can hope that our society adapts to address the systemic challenges created the persistence of economic, political, and social disparities. In the meantime, however, nonprofits fill the void, and that weighty responsibility requires effective risk management.

This book has noted that incrementalism and continuous process improvement—the *lean* in Lean Risk Management—helps develop learning organizations. Over time, team members speak up about what worries and excites them. In that way, this book is a call not just for risk management but also shared accountability and shared responsibility.

For those who hesitate to begin Lean Risk Management, ask them if they think perils disappear simply because they wear a blindfold. Lean Risk Management does not prevent all crises and disasters, and no system will capture every possible opportunity for upside improvement. But, by being radically candid and curious about what is really going on in your nonprofit, focusing on the few issues of greatest importance, and then taking the next reasonable response to those issues, your organization can achieve much greater resilience.

Is there more to be done? Absolutely. As you have learned, Lean Risk Management is a method and practice, not an event. But right now, you have all the tools you need to start down that path.

# APPENDIX

# 1

# 50 Reasons Why It Is Hard to Run a Nonprofit

Most nonprofits perform extraordinarily well with the resources they have. The exceptions noted in Chapter 1 demonstrate, by their relative infrequency, that most nonprofits manage to gather critical financial resources, maintain and grow their staffs, work relatively effectively with volunteer board members, train and supervise volunteers, deal with needy and risky service recipients, grapple with competition, maintain public trust, respond to changes in markets, keep funders informed, and deal with the wide variety of stakeholders.

Given that nonprofits do so well under such circumstances, why worry about the sector? This appendix provides the answer—50 answers, in fact. If anyone doubts your argument that your nonprofit needs to devote time, energy, or money to risk management, give them this appendix and ask them if they face the same conditions in their line of work. (Although this list refers principally to social services nonprofits, the same dynamics tend to apply with other nonprofits.)

### Money Worries

1. **Underfunding.** Most nonprofits do not have sufficient resources for all the activities they wish to perform. The dynamic here is different from a traditional for-profit business. With a for-profit business, insufficient funds may lead to either outright failure or failure to capture all potentially available revenues. The for-profit business may go under because it does not have sufficient resources. It may leave potential money on the table because it cannot meet all the demand for its goods and services. For the typical nonprofit, however, the dynamics are different. Nonprofit employees are not working principally for economic profit but rather some perception of the public good. Although a failure to bring insufficient resources may lead to a failure of the business, more dollars do not necessarily equate to greater comfort and security for the organization. Each additional dollar could serve many additional needy customers.[1] The demand is ever present, and that demand is presented by people who, according to the nonprofit itself, otherwise are going to go without. The question is not whether someone will buy another television or blender; it is whether someone will get the food, clothing, shelter, education resources, or other critical goods and services that can make a material difference in their lives. This sense of bottomless need can create challenging dynamics.

2. **Immediate needs over sustainability.** Because each additional dollar could serve additional needy customers now, it is difficult for a nonprofit to invest in long-term sustainability. It may be hard to rationalize the purchase of new computers when a child may go hungry. When the question is whether to bring on an additional staff member or serve 50 more women on a domestic violence hotline, the organization may be tempted to simply stretch existing staff more thinly. A nonprofit may reasonably believe that it has insufficient resources to spend on infrastructure, including basic management tasks.

3. **Starvation cycle.** In their seminal 2009 article in the *Stanford Social Innovation Review*, Ann Goggins Gregory and Don Howard identified a perverse dynamic in the nonprofit world that they labeled the "starvation cycle."[2] The cycle begins with funders who do not understand the resources it takes to run a nonprofit—particularly the overhead resources not specifically tied to specific programs. Nonprofits feel the need to conform to those expectations to secure funding. Thus, nonprofits both underspend on infrastructure and underreport that spending. Underspending and underreporting ratify funders' unrealistic expectations. As a result, the squeeze on infrastructure funding becomes ever more acute.

4. **Guarded communications.** Because the nonprofit feels threatened by funders who do not want to spend on non-programmatic functions, the nonprofit may feel unwilling to be fully candid with funders. This can lead nonprofits to gloss over problems (or, more bluntly, fail to report them) in funding applications, heightening uncertainty about what it takes to run the organization.[3] It may also lead nonprofits to undervalue or discourage the development of metrics, because metrics suggest performance targets for which nonprofits may then be held accountable.

5. **Scarcity mindset.** A nonprofit can find itself caught in a hand-to-mouth scarcity mindset. The world can look like a zero-sum game, in which any other organization's gain means a loss to the nonprofit. This scarcity mindset undermines morale and inhibits the ability of the organization to identify and take advantage of opportunities when they appear. The same mindset can inhibit fruitful sharing of best practices (and lessons learned) with peer organizations.

6. **Hands perpetually outstretched.** The nonprofit can find itself perpetually fundraising, always with a hand outstretched for one more dollar. "The reality is that non-program dollars are hard to come by, which means that organizations can barely cover ordinary administration and infrastructure costs, let alone use funding to thoughtfully, strategically plan for growth and change."[4]

7. **Mission creep.** In seeking funds, the nonprofit may suffer from mission creep, expanding services and programs in new directions in part because some funder has stated that those initiatives will be funded.[5] Rather than focusing on what they do well and improving the efficiency and effectiveness of those core programs, nonprofits may be tempted to expand beyond their current programmatic activities if they can capture additional revenues.

8. **Donor base squeeze.** Many nonprofits complain that they are losing traditional donors or are finding it hard to identify new donors.

9. **Lack of reserves.** Nonprofits tend to have low reserves of potential cash to cover potential shortfalls and crises. In a 2015 survey, fewer than 50 percent of respondents stated that they had cash reserves of three months or more, and more than 10 percent reported less than one month of cash reserves.[6]

10. **Challenges from new models of revenue generation.** Over the past few decades, nonprofits have begun generating significantly more revenue from commercial income, including sales of products and services and other fees. Income from such services rose "64 percent in real dollar terms between 1997 and 2007."[7] The rise of new models of revenue generation may lead to new demands on an executive director and staff, who must account for this revenue, perform administrative functions that are not traditionally within most nonprofits' core competencies, and justify that revenue to uninformed or skeptical donors who may be leery of nonprofits as a revenue-generating entities.

11. **Short-term focus/aspirational planning.** Many nonprofits engage in strategic planning, but those plans may gather dust because they do not comport with present realities or account for reasonable contingencies.

## Technology Concerns

12. **Outmoded technology.** As a result of the starvation cycle, chronic underfunding, and a general disincentive to spend money on anything other than end user services, nonprofits

tend to be many cycles behind the latest computer technology and other modern equipment. It is not unusual to see a nonprofit using computers that are a decade old, running software that is two or three versions out-of-date, calling people on outmoded telephones, and forcing employees to bring and use their own technology resources to keep up with current demands.

13. **Cyber threats.** Largely because of outmoded technology and lack of funds for communication infrastructure, nonprofits are particularly vulnerable to cybercrime. Although sensitive donor financial information is one potential target (as with the Utah Food Bank described in Chapter 1), nonprofits may also hold sensitive digital data respecting their service populations. Health nonprofits may have sensitive health data. Domestic violence organizations may have name and address information that could be used by abusers. Mental health professionals may have sensitive information about their patients' condition. These data may reside on computer platforms that are vulnerable to attack.

## Staffing and Motivation Challenges

14. **Lack of necessary redundancy.** Nonprofits tend to be staffed more parsimoniously than their for-profit counterparts. Whereas in for-profit organizations staff strive to have redundancy at critical paths to make sure customers' needs are always met, many nonprofits don't have "dundancy" in the first place.. Staff members may wear many hats and perform many tasks, and staff are often required to work outside their areas of expertise to contribute to pressing organizational needs.

15. **Lack of clear progress.** Because the demand for services is so high, nonprofit employees sometimes must "'take it on faith' that the work they are doing day to day is contributing to a larger, more important goal."[8] In contrast to for-profit employees, who can see the results of their efforts in intuitive terms of financial benchmarks and returns to shareholders, nonprofit employees may feel like Sisyphus. The rock is always there to push.

16. **Projects may fall through cracks.** "From antiquated technology to bureaucratic red tape, working at a nonprofit can be downright exasperating. Employees are asked to do more work with fewer resources, create miracles on a daily basis, and satisfy competing interests."[9] Because they are stretched thin and often required to contribute to areas outside their core competencies, nonprofit employees face the fact that important projects get pushed off or neglected.

17. **High stakes.** Compared to many for-profit businesses, nonprofit employees may feel their failures more profoundly. "Consider the difference between losing a few percent off your stock price and losing a mentored young person to drugs. Stakes are simply higher when you are dealing with a cause close to your heart."[10] Nonprofit employees therefore must either create a hard shell of resilience or suffer vicariously along with those they serve.

18. **Overwork and burnout.** A Brookings Institute survey found that 73 percent of nonprofit workers agreed that it was "easy to burn out in their jobs" and that "they always have too much work to do."[11] Nonprofit employees were 10 percent more likely than for-profit employees to say that their organization lacked the resources necessary to perform their jobs well. "Some studies state that as many as 75 percent of executive directors may leave their jobs within the next five years. Other research predicts the nonprofit sector will need to find an additional 640,000 new executives—2.4 times the number currently employed—over the next decade or it will experience a leadership shortfall and a dangerous destabilization of nonprofits as vacating executive directors leave positions unfilled."[12]

19. **Job dissatisfaction.** A 2011 survey of 3,500 nonprofit employees in New York City and Washington, DC, found that 70 percent were dissatisfied with their current jobs, leading 25 percent of them to consider looking for a job outside the nonprofit world.[13] Many workers reported a lack of "respect, trust, and support by management," and more than 60 percent of respondents in both cities reported that their work was not valued sufficiently. Such surveys suggest that job dissatisfaction is, if anything, more prevalent in the nonprofit sector than the for-profit sector,

where job satisfaction stood at 48.3 percent for the entire US population in 2014.[14]

20. **Lower compensation.** Although there is some ambiguity in the data about whether nonprofit salaries actually lag for-profit salaries, nonprofit employees clearly perceive a gap between nonprofit salaries and for-profit salaries for comparable positions.[15] Nonprofit employees may feel that they are working for some higher purpose, but "no matter how much 'psychic income' a nonprofit worker gets from doing work he or she loves, it doesn't pay the rent."[16] Lower compensation may in turn lead to staff attrition and a perpetual need for hiring and training of new personnel. Although creative alternative compensation structures, including flextime and telecommuting, may alleviate some of these burdens, such responses pose their own additional administrative challenges.

21. **Lack of training and development.** Nonprofit employees tend to receive fewer resources for training and development than their for-profit peers.[17] The issue is especially challenging in smaller nonprofits:

> [Smaller nonprofits] usually have flat hierarchies that provide little in the way of career advancement. Resources are notoriously scant, forcing them to operate so close to the margins that they are unable to invest sufficiently in their professional infrastructure. Furthermore, smaller organizations rarely have dedicated human resources staff to provide employees with the same benefits as larger organizations. Often the traditional human resources functions become an additional burden of the executive director or one more task for an "office manager" type of employee. The combination of poor human resource administration, anemic benefits, few opportunities for career advancement, reports of burnout, and perceptions of an adequate pay can hamper an organization's ability to attract and retain talent.[18]

22. **Limited career advancement.** Surveys show that nonprofit employees consistently report that "there [are] few opportunities for advancement or career ladders available to them."[19] Nonprofits promote from within at a rate less than half of their for-profit counterparts.[20] Nonprofit employees thus often find that they must exit their current organization to advance their careers.

## Board Issues

Nonprofit board members are ordinarily volunteers who serve without financial compensation. This presents numerous potential issues for an organization.

23. **Relative competence.** Nonprofit boards almost always serve without compensation. In lieu of a financial incentive, board members are driven instead by a desire to advance the mission, as well as perhaps an understandable desire to enhance their standing in the community through nonprofit service. As a result, board performance suffers. A 2014 survey of nonprofit board members showed that most members did not believe their board was experienced, almost half thought board members were not engaged, and more than a quarter judged that their peers did not have a strong awareness and under-standing of the nonprofit's mission and strategy.[21]

24. **Lack of board governance expertise.** Nonprofit board members rarely come to their position with substantial experience about the proper operation of a nonprofit board. Although nonprofits will occasionally recruit lawyers or businesspeople who have served on other boards, a nonprofit board member often does not know the basics of effective board operations. Board members may be unschooled in the rules of order and may not know their legal obligations. Too often, board members do not receive such training.

25. **Challenging board dynamics.** A nonprofit board also creates challenging dynamics for the executive director/CEO. A for-profit board is characterized by three elements: the board is composed of peers (ordinarily CEOs of other companies or those of similar stations), the CEO is ordinarily the board chair,

and the board has a common basis for determining success (monetary performance).[22] None of those factors tends to hold true in a nonprofit board. Board members may be of very different status and experience from each other and may not be true peers of the executive director. The executive director or CEO of the nonprofit is rarely if ever the board chair. The metrics by which success is measured may be amorphous or nonexistent.

26. **Difficulties policing the board.** Because board members are usually volunteers, it is difficult for an executive director and staff to motivate board members to follow through on their commitments. Staff has no financial lever to apply. Furthermore, nonprofits hesitate to "fire" underperforming board members. Such underperformers may be strong advocates for a nonprofit's issues in the community. They may be significant funders. These dynamics make it challenging to stimulate action by distracted board members or remove troublemakers.[23] As a result, an organization may consistently underperform because of board members who antagonize their peers, fail to attend, or pursue individual agendas at the expense of the organization.

## Volunteer Challenges

Nonprofits often use volunteers for operational activities, which can also create significant challenges not faced within the for-profit community.

27. **Volunteer danger.** Volunteers may be exposed to dangers while working at the nonprofit. This could range from simple slip-and-fall dangers to more specific concerns relating to the service populations or the location of volunteer activities.

28. **Volunteer errors.** Volunteers may commit errors while working on behalf of a nonprofit. As with volunteer board members, it may be more difficult to police volunteer errors, especially errors by otherwise committed, well-meaning, or influential volunteers.

29. **Cost of volunteer guidelines, training, and supervision.** Although volunteers may enable a nonprofit to perform a

greater amount of services than it would without volunteers, that work comes at a cost. The organization must expend resources to draft necessary administrative materials to guide volunteer behavior, train volunteers, and supervise them in the field, reducing the availability of staff resources for other activities.

## Challenges Related to Service Populations

Most nonprofits exist to serve some vulnerable population. In fact, nonprofits routinely serve children, the elderly, minority populations, the homeless, immigrants, veterans, the mentally ill, or the mentally disabled. The plight of such service communities can create challenging dynamics.

30. **Guilt.** Related to issue 2, nonprofit staff may feel guilty about using resources for any expenditure other than direct services for the target population. The nonprofit may put its own long-term sustainability at risk by over-committing resources to current needy service recipients.

31. **Endless sea of need.** Similarly, the nonprofit staff may feel discouragement in the face of what seems to be perpetual, unsolvable societal problems.

32. **Staff danger.** Nonprofits often work with individuals who are more risky to serve because they live in circumstances that attract hardship or they engage in risky behaviors.[24] This may be particularly true when a service population is poor, mentally challenged, or has engaged in illegal conduct. If an organization serves ex-felons, drug users, or the homeless, for example, staff and volunteers who interact with such user populations may find themselves in dangerous physical and emotional circumstances, or they may at least worry about an enhanced threat of personal harm.

33. **Staff recruiting and retention.** It may be more challenging to recruit and retain personnel to work with populations that are engaged in risky behavior or live in dangerous conditions. There may be fewer true believers, and even true believers may burn out more rapidly in such difficult provider circumstances.

34. **Enhanced threat of failure.** When dealing with particularly challenged populations, a nonprofit staff may find it difficult to achieve "success" outcomes no matter how hard they try. If they do achieve "success," it may be on exceptionally long timetables. The sense that a target population is doomed to fail notwithstanding the nonprofit's best efforts can undermine staff morale, board engagement, and funding.

35. **Funding unpopular causes.** Nonprofits often exist to fill the needs of societally unpopular end user populations. Precisely because the target population is unpopular, however, it may be hard to raise money for such people. It may be difficult, for example, to garner funding for immigrants in xenophobic times, or to channel resources toward homelessness when a community does not wish to acknowledge such people in the streets or believes the homeless are victims solely of their own poor choices.

36. **Additional regulatory hurdles.** When dealing with certain vulnerable target populations, a nonprofit may be required to perform additional background checks or provide additional training to field competent personnel.

## Competition

37. **For-profit competitors.** Nonprofits face increasing competition from for-profit cause-based organizations. For-profit businesses have certain intrinsic advantages over nonprofits. They can raise capital more swiftly by using equity markets, so they can take advantage of emerging trends more rapidly. Their access to equity also enables them to raise the large amounts of capital sometimes required to apply technology to social challenges.[25] For-profits may also skim the easiest cases from a needy population, leaving only the harder cases for nonprofits.[26] Thus, nonprofits may end up serving those members of a community who are least susceptible to success and most costly to serve.

38. **Competition for funding from other comparable nonprofits.** Because of the rise of the internet, potential donors are more aware of the variety of nonprofits providing a particular service in a given community or elsewhere. They also are more

aware of the operational activities of each nonprofit. As a result, nonprofits face increasing competition for donor dollars from other comparable nonprofits.[27] A donor who once would have given money to a local food bank may instead be confronted with choices of other food banks in the region that profess greater "efficiency" or "effectiveness" with donor dollars, regional or national organizations that may address hunger at a more broad-based, structural level, or other options that they would not have known about before the rise of modern communications technology.

39. **Competition from larger nonprofits.** Smaller nonprofits face particular competition from their larger peers. Large nonprofits have greater flexibility with resources, enabling them to make significant technological capital investments.[28] They are also often able to provide more training and development for employees and offer greater upward career mobility.[29]

### Political Worries

40. **Viewed as special interests.** The nonprofit sector has faced an unrelenting challenge since the 1970s from commentators in conservative political circles, who have accused nonprofits of being essentially just one more special interest seeking government money to "feather their own nests."[30] Additionally, because of sporadic high-profile failures and abuses, public support for nonprofits is not nearly as robust as it was some decades ago; to the contrary, some contend that "America's nonprofit institutions are delicately balanced on a knife edge of public support, with most people willing to grant them the benefit of the doubt, but with a strong undercurrent of uncertainty and concern."[31]

### Compliance Issues

41. Quite apart from regulations specific to their status as not-for-profit entities, nonprofits face a **host of regulatory considerations**, from zoning, to health and safety, to anti-discrimination and others. (For a taste of those issues, see Appendix 5.)

## "Market" Failures

In classical economics, nonprofits are often justified as existing to deal with failures in traditional markets. Nonprofits aggregate resources on behalf of causes and populations that might be ignored by traditional market forces. They protect and advance public goods such as education and environmental sustainability. These public goods benefit an entire community, but such goods are undervalued because they are intangible. By aggregating resources through a common cause, nonprofits address market deficiencies.

Although those principles are no doubt true, nonprofits also fail to conform to traditional, for-profit market behavior in ways that pose risks to themselves, their causes, and their communities.

42. **Just hanging on.** If a for-profit business fails to perform its activities as effectively as competitors, it will go out of business. Nonprofits rarely do. So long as a nonprofit can persuade a few donors to fund an effort, it may limp along for years after its value to the community has run its course.

43. **Founder's syndrome.** The problem of the lingering nonprofit may be compounded by the peculiar dynamics within the nonprofit sector. Nonprofits are often founded by a powerful personality who continues to exert substantial influence over the organization for many years. Although the founder's determination and ability to organize others toward a common objective doubtless helps the organization get on its feet, a nonprofit may find it difficult to remove such a powerful and charismatic figure as the nonprofit confronts new circumstances. Founder's syndrome tends to manifest in four symptoms: "The first is a sense of grandiosity—that the organization is the founder's, and it exists to serve his or her ego (or pocketbook). The second is an inability to delegate—poor management on the part of the founder. The third is an inability to make a smooth transition from the founder to new leadership. And the fourth is an unwavering dedication to the original vision for the organization."[32] Such symptoms can make it difficult to move beyond the startup stage of nonprofit into a more sustainable growth path. Indeed, the transition from founding

executive director to their successor may be one of the most traumatic points in the nonprofit life cycle.

44. **Resistance to consolidation.** During the Great Recession, mergers in for-profit industries accelerated. Nonprofits, however, did not see the same consolidation. To the contrary, nonprofit mergers remained flat.[33] Research suggests that nonprofits persistently resist mergers because of challenges in aligning boards, fitting in senior staff, aligning missions, and finding funding for due diligence and execution of mergers. This resistance to consolidation may lead to misuse of resources for needy populations, duplication of efforts within a community, and disputes about turf and priority.

45. **Missed opportunities.** Nonprofits often complain that it is difficult to get the message out to funders and potential funders about what they do, how they do it, why it is important, and how it matters in their communities. Research supports this common intuition.[34] This means many funders simply do not know what many nonprofits do. Worthy programs may go underfunded or may wither away because potential funders are not aware of the activities or their beneficial effects.

46. **Misunderstandings.** Funders may not understand how a nonprofit intends to execute on its theory of change. This can lead to uncertainty about whether to fund, unrealistic expectations, and other problems.

47. **Misallocation of scarce resources.** If funders do not know what different nonprofits do, it is difficult for them to make funding decisions effectively.

48. **Just whom does the nonprofit serve?** Traditional, for-profit businesses perform their activities to make money for their owners. For nonprofits, the stakeholders are much more diffuse. They include current service beneficiaries, current donors, current board members, current volunteers, and current staff. They also include, however, future service recipients, who will never receive the nonprofit's benefits if the organization does not sustain its operations into the future. They include future

volunteers, future staff, and future board members. Stakeholders also include regulatory authorities, who must ensure that the nonprofit is conforming to community standards. And stakeholders additionally include the community itself, which has some interest in how the nonprofit fits into an overall scheme for providing social goods. As a result, it can be challenging to determine the true best interests of a nonprofit. For example, should the nonprofit focus predominantly on current service users, even if that endangers long-term sustainability? Researcher Regina Herzlinger answers: "In general, a nonprofit should not sacrifice present generations of users for the benefit of future ones and vice versa. When a charity saves an excessively large proportion of its resources to help future users, it denies benefits to present users. Conversely, when it consumes virtually all its assets to serve present users, it denies the benefits of the organization's services to future users."[35] But where does one strike that balance, and how does a nonprofit determine issues at the margin? If the nonprofit wishes to take account of future beneficiaries, how does it determine their identities? Furthermore, how does it determine the interests of a diverse portfolio of current donors? To the extent future funders interests may be implicated, how does the nonprofit account for those additional potential interests? These ambiguities make it challenging for a nonprofit staff and board of directors to execute on their basic legal duties of care, loyalty, and obedience.

## Planning and Visioning Issues

49. **Failure to keep apprised of important context.** When a nonprofit is perpetually stretched thin, it is challenging to devote time and resources to keeping apprised of industry developments and economic forces that may affect current and future operations.

50. **Failure to articulate, apply, and police values.** Although many nonprofits justifiably pride themselves on being mission-driven organizations with strong values, many nonprofits do not pause

to articulate those values and incorporate them into everyday practices and procedures.

* * *

In short, nonprofits face a panoply of threats. As a result, any tool that promises greater agility and sustainability should be particularly attractive to nonprofit leaders. Risk management is that tool.

# 2

---

# Questions to Use During Risk Inventories

THIS APPENDIX PROVIDES questions that can stimulate discussion and evaluation and identify risks in every function of your organization, as well as external forces that could affect the organization over time. You do not have to answer every question, but if you are having a hard time identifying issues, these inquiries may help.

This appendix can also be used as you implement a risk cycle to generate additional ideas for exploration of threats and opportunities.

## Operations

The operations of an organization consist of the ways in which the organization conveys value to its customers or clients.

*Value Streams and Processes*

Nonprofits should think of themselves as providing one or more value streams—that is, processes through which their customer is provided with goods or services that provide value. We evaluate operations through the lens of those value streams.

1. What are our value streams?
2. Who are the customers we serve in each value stream?
3. How much revenue does each value stream generate?
4. How has this changed over time?
5. How do we expect revenues to change in each value stream in the foreseeable future?
6. Within each value stream, what does the customer want?
7. How do we know this?
8. In each value stream, are our customers satisfied with the value they are receiving from us?
9. How do we know this?
10. Should we provide additional or different value streams to our customers?
11. Have we documented each of our major processes within each value stream?
12. For each process, have we evaluated whether it could be improved?
13. What two or three steps could we take in this quarter that would materially improve our performance in one or more of our value streams from the customer's perspective?

Some value streams do not have external customers. Talent management, for instance, serves every other functional area of the organization but does not have external customers. Those internal value streams deserve evaluation, too.

1. Have we identified our internal (support) value streams?

2. Are our internal customers satisfied with the value provided in those internal value streams? (For example, is operations satisfied with the employees hired and developed through talent management?)

3. How do we know this?

4. What two or three steps could we take this quarter that would materially improve our performance in one or more of our internal value streams?

## Vendors

1. Who are our major external vendors?

2. What contracts govern those relationships?

3. Are we satisfied with the terms?

4. Have we considered outsourcing any of our internal support functions?

5. Why or why not?

6. Have we considered insourcing any functions that we have previously outsourced?

7. Why or why not?

8. Do we have any agreements for financing with any vendors?

9. Do we have any letters of credit?

10. Do we have any loans outstanding?

11. Are we satisfied with the terms of our financing and debt?

## Volunteers

1. Do we staff any of our operations using volunteers?

2. What sort of background check do we perform on volunteers?

3. Do we have a formal training process for our volunteers?

4. How do we ensure that volunteers follow their training?

5. How do we supervise our volunteers?

6. How do we discipline or course-correct volunteers if they fail to perform as required?

7. Have we evaluated whether we have the proper insurance coverages given how we use volunteers?

8. How do we acknowledge our volunteers to make them feel supported and wanted?

## Facilities

1. Do we have any facility leases?

2. Are we satisfied with the terms?

3. Is the landlord responsive to our needs?

4. If we own our facility(ies), have we reflected on the long-term plans for the property and evaluated our options?

5. Do we have any actual or potential disputes relating to our facilities?

6. Are there any physical hazards or dangers in or near our workplace?

## Trade Secrets and Intellectual Property

1. Do we have any trade secrets?

2. Do we have appropriate confidentiality agreements in place?

3. Do we have any intellectual property?

4. Is our intellectual property properly protected?

## Competitors

1. Who are our competitors?

2. How do our major competitors differentiate themselves from us?

3. How do we differentiate ourselves from our major competitors?

4. How is the competitive landscape changing over time?

## *Outside Forces*

1. What economic forces principally affect our value streams?

2. If economic circumstances change (for better or worse), how would the organization respond?

3. What social or political forces principally affect our value streams?

4. If social or political forces change (for better or worse), how would the organization respond?

5. If competitive forces changed, how would the organization respond?

## *Metrics*

1. What key performance indicators (KPIs) do we use to measure our operations?

2. How do we gather data to determine whether we are meeting our KPIs?

3. Based on those metrics, how do we measure up?

4. Do we foresee any changes in the next year?

## Information Technology

1. When was the last time we performed an assessment of whether our hardware and software meet our needs?

2. Do we have any software that is outdated and no longer supported by the vendor?

3. Do we use more than one software program or application to perform similar functions within the organization?

4. If so, should we choose one or the other of those programs, instead of using both?

5. Are we satisfied with each software program we use?

6. How do we provide computer hardware and software support to our team?

7. Are we satisfied with that support?

8. Where does our electronic data reside—on servers, the cloud, or the hard drives of individual computers owned by our nonprofit?

9. Do our employees and/or volunteers use their personal computers to access our data?

10. Do our employees and/or volunteers create and store files on their personal computers?

11. How often do we back up our data?

12. Do we have a data loss and recovery plan to be able to quickly get back in business after a loss?

13. How do we confirm that our information is secure?

14. Do we have some sort of data loss protection program in place to prevent unauthorized disclosure of sensitive data to those outside the organization?

15. When was last time we had an outside assessment of our telecommunications equipment?

16. When was the last time we had an outside vendor perform a threat assessment for our IT systems?

## Finance

The finance function involves how an organization accounts for its operations, reports results for those operations, and maintains money and related assets.

### Internal Accounting

1. How do we perform our accounting?

2. Are we satisfied with our accounting procedures?

3. Do we perform a monthly closing of our books?

4. How is that performed, and who ensures that it is done?

5. Do we perform bank reconciliations?

6. What internal financial controls (e.g., financial procedures manual, segregation of responsibilities) do we have to ensure that our books are sound?

7. Are we comfortable that our internal financial controls are sufficient?

8. What internal financial reports do we generate?

9. Are those reports sufficient for our purposes?

10. How and where are our accounting records kept?

11. How are they archived or shredded?

12. How often is filing performed?

## Taxes

1. Do we use an outside tax preparer?

2. Are we satisfied with the tax preparer's performance?

3. What safeguards are in place to ensure tax compliance?

## Banking

1. What banking relationships do we have?

2. Are we satisfied with those relationships?

3. When was the last time we sought advice from our banker?

4. Do we use our banker as a trusted advisor?

## Budgeting

1. Do we have a budget?

2. Who is involved in developing the budget?

3. Who approves the budget?

4. What is the timing of each major step in the budget cycle?

5. Do we reconcile our actual costs to our budget?

## Auditing

1. Do we need an audit?

2. Who performs the audit function?

3. Are we satisfied with the auditors' performance?

4. Have the auditors' reports and management letters identified any material weaknesses in our accounting systems or controls?

5. If so, have we followed up on those issues?

6. When was the last time we switched auditors to get a new set of eyes on our books?

## Payroll

1. Who performs payroll?

2. Are we satisfied with the payroll process?

3. Have any issues arisen about payroll?

## Receivables

1. How often does the organization prepare invoices?

2. How does the organization ensure payment?

3. How does the organization keep records?

4. Who reviews and follows up on receivables?

5. Does the organization have significant cash receipts?

6. How are cash receipts documented and processed?

7. Are there any issues about the security of cash receipts?

## Payables

1. For purchases, are purchase orders required?

2. Who has the authority to make purchases?

3. How are purchases approved and documented?

4. Who opens and responds to invoices?

5. Are invoices properly input into the financial reporting system?

6. How do we handle cash disbursements?

7. Do we have a petty cash system?

8. How is petty cash monitored?

9. How are employee expenses documented and processed?

## Investments and Asset Management

1. Who is responsible for managing investment accounts?

2. Are we satisfied with our investment performance?

3. How do we account for capital equipment?

4. Do we have employee retirement accounts or financial benefits?

5. When was last time we sought an assessment from an outside professional about employee retirement accounts?

6. Are employee financial benefits properly accounted for?

7. Do we have a financial reserve?

8. How do we monitor whether our financial reserve is appropriate given the organization's current and projected needs?

## Talent Management

The term *talent management* includes recruiting, hiring, developing, regulating, and terminating the employment of workers.

1. How do we assess the talent needs for our current operations and operations in the foreseeable future?

2. Are we satisfied with those processes?

3. What processes do we have in place for the professional development of our workforce?

4. Are we satisfied with those processes?

5. By what metrics do we gauge employee engagement and satisfaction?

6. By those measures, how are we doing?

7. Does the organization have a healthy culture?

8. What are the hallmarks of our organization's culture?

9. Have we consciously decided what culture we want within our organization?

10. Do we have any current disputes among particular workers or groups within our organization?

11. How are those disputes being addressed?

12. Are we satisfied with the way we address and resolve disputes?

13. Do we have anyone in the organization who works more than eight hours per day or more than 40 hours per week?

14. If so, have we spoken with a professional to ensure that we are treating those workers properly under the law?

15. Do we have any workers whom we consider independent contractors?

16. If so, have we spoken to a professional to determine whether independent contractors work within relevant independent contractor guidelines?

17. Do we have any underage workers?

18. If so, have we spoken with a professional to ensure that such workers are being treated properly under the relevant law?

19. Do we have a standard process for employment searches?
    a. Do we ask for and check references?
    b. Do we ask for and review résumés?
    c. Do we perform a background check?

20. Do we ensure that we are acting in a nondiscriminatory manner?

21. Do we have an employee policy manual or handbook?

22. When was last time the employee handbook was updated?

23. How do we ensure that employees understand and follow the employee handbook?

24. How do we protect against discrimination and harassment in the workplace?

25. Do we have written job descriptions?

26. When were job descriptions last reviewed and updated?

27. When did we last confirm that each worker knows their job description?

28. Do we document promotions and disciplinary actions?

29. What documentation do we require for voluntary and involuntary terminations?

30. Do we perform exit interviews?

31. Do we have employment contracts for key employees?

32. Have we performed a business skills inventory, itemizing each of the skills of each of our team members?

## Reputation Management

Reputation management includes both marketing and public relations. The function involves how an organization is perceived, how it wants to be perceived, and how it attempts to influence perceptions.

1. What metrics do we use to gauge our reputation in the community?

2. Under those metrics, how are we doing?

3. What metrics do we use to gauge awareness of our organization in the community?

4. Under those metrics, how are we doing?

5. How do we currently educate potential customers about what we offer?

6. What metrics do we use to measure our efforts to educate customers on what we offer?

7. Are we satisfied with those efforts?

8. Do we have any efforts in place to raise awareness or modify perceptions of our goods and services in various markets to create new potential customers?

9. What metrics do we use to measure those efforts?

10. Are we satisfied with those efforts?

11. Do we have a crisis management plan in place in case an issue arises that could cause reputational damage to the organization?

12. When was the last time we reviewed our crisis management plan?

13. Do we use any forms of social media?

14. Who monitors social media use?

15. Do we have a social media policy?

16. What economic, social, political, and community trends can we identify that might pose threats or create opportunities for the management of our reputation?

## Sales of Goods and Services

Nonprofits may resist the notion that they perform sales functions. Even if you provide goods and services at low or no cost, you are making an exchange of value, raising many relevant (and often neglected) questions.

1. Why do end users of our goods or services "buy" what we provide?

2. What steps do we take to determine precisely what our customers want and how our services meet those preferences?

3. Do we make any monetary sales of goods or services to customers?

4. What form of agreement is used to sell goods and services to customers?

5. What steps do we take to minimize our liability in making sales?

6. Do we extend any warranties?

7. If so, what are the terms?

8. Should they be modified?

9. Do any of our contracts extend credit?

10. How do we check credit before extending credit?

11. What do we do when we are not paid?

12. Have we had any customer disputes in the last year?

13. How are customer disputes resolved?

14. How do we track current and former customers?

15. Do we have a client relationship management (CRM) database?

16. How is our CRM database maintained?

17. Are we satisfied with our CRM's performance?

18. How are our target populations changing?

19. Would we like to see our target populations change over time?

20. How do we compensate our sales personnel?

21. Are sales personnel satisfied with their compensation plan?

22. Do we provide incentives to our sales force?

23. Do we have a sales script for sales personnel?

24. How do we ensure that personnel stick to the sales script?

25. Have we confirmed that our personnel are not making any unsubstantiated claims or promises during our sales process that the organization cannot keep?

26. How, if at all, do we incorporate online activities into our sales process?

27. Are there ways to improve the online experience for our target populations?

## Sales to Donors (Development)

Funders provide nonprofits with money for a variety of reasons, including the desire to alleviate some harm in the community, advance a social agenda, or benefit from the halo effect of charitable acts. As a result, there is an implicit or explicit sales aspect with respect to interactions with donors. The funder is buying something, and that raises issues.

1. Why do donors give us money?

2. How do we know that?

3. How do we measure how we satisfy donor interests?

4. What promises do we make to donors during the development process?

5. Have we confirmed that our personnel are not making any unsubstantiated claims or promises during our development process that the organization cannot keep?

6. Is the number of donors growing or shrinking?

7. What, if anything, does this say about the health of our nonprofit?

8. What other organizations do our donors give money to, and how do we compare to those organizations?

9. Do we believe that our current donor pipeline is sufficient to cover our future organizational needs?

10. How do we know that?

11. How would we respond to a significant increase or decrease in donations?

12. Do we have a funding diversification plan in place?

13. Do we maintain our donor list as a trade secret?

14. Do we maintain our donor prospecting list as a trade secret?

15. How do we protect our donor list?

16. Do we have criteria in place to determine whether we would consider selling our donor list to some other organization?

17. How do we review our donor list and improve it over time?

18. How many mailings or electronic touches do we have with donors per month?

19. Who drafts donor messages?

20. Who approves donor messages?

21. How well does our website serve the development function?

22. How do we compare with peer organizations in the development function?

23. How do we know that?

24. How do we seek donor feedback?

25. Who within our organization is principally involved in the development function?

26. What is the role of each person?

27. Do those roles create any inefficiencies?

28. Is each person performing his or her role adequately?

29. Do we host any events in the development process?

30. Have we checked to make sure we have sufficient insurance for such events?

## Risk Management

Risk management involves how an organization identifies and addresses threats and opportunities.

1. Do we have a risk management program?

2. Who is responsible for supervising the risk management program?

3. What are the components of our risk management program?

4. Have we performed a risk inventory to determine threats and opportunities throughout the organization?

5. Do we use a risk register to capture and prioritize threats and opportunities?

6. Do we review our risk register periodically at staff meetings to assess progress in addressing risks?

7. Do we have an incident log to record accidents and responses?

8. Do we have a process in place to follow up on incidents?

9. Looking at the incidents log, are there any discernible patterns or trends?

10. Is our work environment healthy and safe?

11. What steps have we taken to determine if our work environment is healthy and safe?

12. Do we have a suggestion box or other procedure that employees can use to identify threats and opportunities?

13. If so, how often is that used?

14. How does the organization energize and incentivize employees to identify threats and opportunities that may affect the organization?

15. How do we track industry developments to look for threats and opportunities?

16. Do we have a business continuity plan in place to address emergencies that could affect our ability to perform our activities?

17. How do we build out our network of connections to peers?

18. How do we build out our network beyond our peers?

19. What insurance do we have?

20. When was last time we had an outside professional (besides our current broker) review our insurance policies?

21. How could our internal policies and procedures be articulated, clarified, or simplified to reduce threats to the organization?

22. How could provisions of our recurring contracts be modified to reduce threats to the nonprofit?

23. What processes do we have in place to identify and develop new initiatives that would enhance our offerings or effectiveness?

## Compliance

The compliance function consists of processes and procedures by which an organization ensures that it is following internal guidelines and external regulations.

1. Do we have any pending legal disputes?

2. When was the last time we consulted a lawyer?

3. What was that for?

4. Have we recently considered consulting a lawyer?

5. What for?

6. Do we have an ongoing relationship with an outside attorney whom we pay for services?

7. Are we satisfied with that relationship?

8. What regulatory authorities do we report to (e.g., IRS, state, localities, or subject-specific regulators)?

9. What licenses do we need?

10. Are all licenses current?

11. Have we filed all appropriate papers with all relevant regulatory authorities?

12. Do we have an ethics policy?

13. What steps are taken to ensure that all employees follow the ethics policy?

14. Do we have an employee handbook?

15. What steps are taken to ensure that all employees follow the employee handbook?

16. What is our document retention policy?

17. Do we comply with that policy?

18. Do we receive any funding from outside sources (e.g., governmental, foundation) that require us to comply with reporting or disbursement policies?

19. If so, are we compliant with each requirement?
    (For additional materials relating to compliance, see Appendix 5.)

## Planning and Visioning

Every organization has some idea of where it is going. This book calls these efforts the *planning function*. Most organizations also have taken some steps to identify what they stand for. This book calls these *vision activities*.

### Strategic Plan

1. Do we have a strategic plan?

2. How and when was it adopted?

3. Is it current?

4. Does the plan have metrics by which progress is measured?

5. How often do we compare our results to our plan?

6. What does a comparison of the plan versus actual results tell us about the effectiveness of our planning process?

7. How do we involve staff in planning?

8. Could this be improved?

9. How do we involve senior leadership in planning?

10. Could this be improved?

11. What are our growth projections for the next five years?

12. What is the basis for those projections?

13. What forces external to the organization (e.g., economic, social, environmental) pose a significant threat to the organization's health or viability?

14. What forces pose significant opportunities for our organization?

15. What steps have we taken to identify whether we should merge or partner with one or more other organizations?

16. If a critic were evaluating us, where would that critic rank us relative to our peers?

## Annual Operating Plan

1. Do we have an annual operating plan?

2. How often do we refer to the operating plan?

3. Does the annual operating plan have metrics by which progress is measured?

4. By those metrics, how are we doing?

5. How do we involve staff in the development of the annual operating plan?

6. To what extent do we involve the board in developing the annual operating plan?

7. Looking back over the past three years, how have our annual operating plans compared with what actually happened that year?

8. What does that tell us about our planning process?

## Mission

1. Have we identified the organization's mission?

2. Going back to our articles of incorporation, how does our current mission compare to our original intent?

3. How do we articulate the mission on our website, in our materials for donors, and in the community?

4. How consistently do we advance our mission?

5. If a critic were evaluating us, in what ways would the critic say we were not meeting our mission?

## Values

1. Have we identified our organization's core values?

2. What steps have we taken to convey our core values to employees and ensure that the organization is living its values?

3. Assuming a devil's advocate position, how would a critic contend we are not living our values?

## Governance

The governance function for nonprofits involves how a board of directors interacts with staff and how staff personnel interact with each other.

1. Are our bylaws consistent with our articles of incorporation?

2. When was the last time our bylaws were reviewed by an attorney?

3. Do we comply with our bylaws?

4. How do we train new and existing board members about our bylaws?

5. Have we adopted core board-approved policies on whistle-blowing, conflict of interest, and other issues?

6. Do any of our current business relationships create conflicts of interest for any staff or board members?

7. Do we have a process in place for determining the skills necessary within our board of directors?

8. Do we have a process in place for recruiting new board members who fill those skill sets?

9. Can each of our board members articulate our organization's mission?

10. How do we measure board engagement?

11. Under that measure, how does our board measure up?

12. How do board members interact with each other?

13. Do any tensions or disfunctions among board members need to be addressed?

14. Do we have term limits for board members?

15. Do we enforce board member term limits?

16. Are our board meetings efficient and effective?

17. How could they be improved?

18. Do our board members understand their governance function?

19. How often do we review the governance function with the board?

20. Do we provide regular training and information for our board members?

21. Does our board interact constructively with staff?

22. What improvements should we consider?

23. Do we have an organizational chart for our staff?

24. Does the organization chart reflect how the organization actually performs its functions?

25. Do we have job descriptions for all members of our staff?

26. How do the actual jobs compare with the job descriptions?

27. How does leadership convey important information to the staff?

28. Could this process be improved?

29. How long has the executive director/CEO been in their position?

30. Does this tenure create any challenging dynamics relative to the board (e.g., excessive board deference because of long tenure, excessive board interference because of short tenure)?

31. If senior leadership left the organization tomorrow, how much institutional knowledge would be lost because of sparse documentation of policies, procedures, or other critical information?

## Diversity, Equity, and Inclusion

1. Have we assessed whether and how our organization—including our board, staff leadership, and rank and file—reflects the demographics and interests of the communities it serves?

2. To the extent our organization does not reflect our target communities, what steps are we taking to address those disparities?

3. By what metrics will we measure progress?

4. Have we decided whether and how our organization intends to combat discrimination and racism?

5. If the organization intends to combat discrimination and racism, what steps are we taking?

6. By what metrics will we measure progress?

## Questions for External Context

After examining the various functions of your organization, you will also examine the external context in which your nonprofit operates.

### Political/Governmental Forces

Here, you are looking at issues that arise from the interaction of political forces and governmental agencies.

1. What local political factors influence our organization?

2. What local political factors influence our target population(s)?

3. What state-level political factors influence our organization?

4. What state-level political factors influence our target population(s)?

5. What national political factors influence our organization?

6. What national political factors influence our target population(s)?

7. When was the last time there was a significant shift in local, state, or national politics? In other words, how stable is the

political environment in which our organization and our target population(s) operate?

8. How connected is our nonprofit with those who influence local, state, and national politics?

9. What vulnerabilities or opportunities do these connections (or lack of connections) present?

10. How connected is/are our target population(s) with those who influence local, state, and national politics?

11. What vulnerabilities or opportunities do these connections (or lack of connections) present?

12. Suppose that in the next election the political party not currently in power took over control of the local government. How might that affect our organization?

13. How might that affect our target population(s)?

14. What if the regional or state government changed hands?

15. What if there was a switch at the national level?

## Economic Forces

Your nonprofit may be buffeted by external economic conditions. Relevant questions include the following.

1. How is our local economy doing?

2. What are influencers saying about prospects for the future?

3. How is the regional economy performing?

4. What are predictions for the future?

5. How is the national economy performing?

6. What are people predicting for the future?

7. How might an improvement in the local, regional, or national economy affect our nonprofit?

8. How might a decline in the local, regional, or national economy affect our nonprofit?

9. How might an improvement or a decline in the local, regional, or national economy affect our target population(s)?

10. What would happen to our nonprofit and our target population(s) if unemployment rose by 5 percent in our locality?

11. What would happen to our organization if unemployment fell by 3 percent?

12. What would happen to our nonprofit and our target population(s) if inflation rose by 5 percent in our locality?

13. What would happen if our locality experienced deflation?

14. How many new organizations that could be viewed as competitors have begun operations in our community?

15. How many organizations that could be viewed as competitors have gone out of business in recent years?

16. Suppose we were starting from scratch and trying to create an organization that would compete with our nonprofit. What would we do differently to perform better?

17. How many of those steps can we take now to improve our nonprofit relative to its peers?

## Social Forces

Broad social trends can have a profound influence on organizational resilience, health, and sustainability. Consider these questions.

1. What social trends among gender, age groups, races, and so on, could significantly affect our nonprofit or our target population(s)?

2. Perform a simple online search of predictions of social trends for this year and next year. How might each of those trends affect our nonprofit or our target population(s)?

## Ecological/Environmental/Sustainability Forces

One growing area of potential risk involves an organization's ecological footprint. Consider these issues.

1. How much does our organization affect the environment?

2. Are those impacts positive or negative?

3. What would happen to our organization if regulations changed to increase strictures relating to environmental impact?

4. Do we consider ecological sustainability as part of our impact on the community?

5. What would a critic say about our organization's ecological sustainability efforts?

# APPENDIX

# 3

# Nonprofit Risk Management Policy Templates

A NONPROFIT RISK management policy does not need to be detailed. Here are two simple examples.

## Example 1

The board of directors hereby resolves that [ORGANIZATION] shall implement a risk management process to provide reasonable assurance that the organization in a timely manner identifies threats and opportunities, prioritizes those risks, and responds appropriately to risks, considering available resources. The board delegates to the [TITLE OF ORGANIZATION ED/CEO] the duty to implement this process and document any necessary protocols.

## Example 2

POLICY:    XX.XX
TITLE:     RISK MANAGEMENT POLICY
POLICY:

[ORGANIZATION] shall have a risk management program that ensures that risks, both threats and opportunities, are managed through a routine process to identify, prioritize, respond, and assess/improve as appropriate in a continuous cycle.

## RESPONSIBILITIES:

The board of directors is responsible for implementation of this policy.

The board of directors shall create a risk management subcommittee, who will determine the cadence for board review of highest-priority risks, and report to the board as needed.

The [TITLE OF ORGANIZATION ED/CEO] is responsible for leading the organization's risk management program, establishing a procedure to execute a risk management process in the organization, and ensuring all staff understand risk management and their individual responsibilities per the procedure.

## GENERAL PROVISIONS:

Risk management is an essential function for reducing threats and leveraging opportunities. In assessing the effectiveness of its risk management program, the risk management subcommittee will conduct a semiannual program evaluation. This evaluation is composed of the following:

A. Risk Status Report. [ORGANIZATION] shall maintain a risk register as the principal tool for tracking prioritized risks, both threats and opportunities. The top risks and actions taken will be shared semiannually with the board in a risk status report.

B. Routine Review and Monitoring.
    1. The board may, from time to time, assess threats and opportunities to the organization that will be added to the risk register for prioritization and possible action by staff.
    2. [TITLE OF ORGANIZATION ED/CEO] will ensure that new risks are added to the register with an appropriate cadence, and all risks are prioritized to ensure they are addressed if and when appropriate.

Adopted:

[NAME], Chairman, [ORGANIZATION] Board of Directors

[DATE]

# APPENDIX

# 4

## Fundamental Risk Management Elements (FRaMEs)

MANY NONPROFITS DO not yet have formal risk management programs. Still, most nonprofits use some forms of risk management every day. This book refers to these practices and documents as *fundamental risk management elements* (FRaMEs). If you are like most nonprofits, you probably use some of these FRaMEs, but you may be interested in whether you have them all and whether you are getting full value out of each tool. So what are these FRaMEs? They include the following.

### Official Documents and Policies
- **Articles of incorporation.** A nonprofit's articles of incorporation are filed in its state of incorporation. This document lists the initial purpose of the organization and its original board of directors.

175

The risk management function of articles of incorporation are simple: periodically, the organization should review its articles to confirm that its current mission and programs conform to its articles. If the nonprofit finds any inconsistencies, the organization should either file revised articles of incorporation or modify its practices to constrain its behavior according to the articles.

- **Bylaws.** Bylaws set forth how a nonprofit board of directors will perform its functions, including whether and how it delegates authority to staff. A nonprofit should periodically confirm that its board continues to perform consistent with its bylaws. It should also periodically explore whether any bylaws should be modified to enhance work performance.
- **Ethics policy signed by all employees.** An ethics policy sets out a nonprofit's commitment to abiding by basic business practices. Having employees sign the ethics policy periodically reinforces the importance of ethical conduct and provides a means of accountability if someone violates the policy.
- **Whistleblower policy.** The whistleblower policy provides employees with a safe feedback mechanism to report potential wrongdoing without facing repercussions.
- **Conflict-of-interest policy.** A conflict-of-interest policy reduces the likelihood that board members or staff members will put their own interests before those of the organization.
- **Sexual harassment prevention policy.** A sexual harassment prevention policy reinforces an organization's commitment to creating a safe and productive work environment.

## Core Procedural Documents

- **Employee handbook.** An employee handbook sets out elements of employee obligations and benefits. A handbook can resolve critical ambiguities about permissible employee conduct.
- **Written job descriptions.** Written job descriptions provide clarity during hiring, training, performance reviews, discipline, and (if necessary) termination.
- **Segregation of job duties.** Segregation of job duties is an important control on aspects of the financial function of the organization.

For instance, a nonprofit might provide that one person opens envelopes containing checks while another records them. It might provide that one person prepares pay information for payroll while another person approves those calculations.

■ **Policy and procedure manuals.** Policy and procedure manuals spell out how an organization performs basic processes. Such manuals help to standardize conduct and resolve ambiguities. They also provide a baseline for potential innovations.

## Core Planning Documents

■ **Strategic planning process.** A strategic planning process provides a critical risk management function by setting direction for the organization and metrics by which overall performance will be measured.

■ **Advocacy plan.** An advocacy plan sets forth a nonprofit's goals for supporting its mission in the community, the strategies it will use to accomplish such goals, and the expected outcomes for those strategies. Such a plan supports risk management by articulating such core issues as to whether and how the organization will give voice to potential social and political issues without violating any applicable rules with respect to charitable organization advocacy.

■ **Annual operating plan.** An annual operating plan gives life to an organization's budget by describing expected activities, milestones, and metrics. Similar to strategic planning, an annual operating plan serves a risk management function by forcing team members to think about the future concretely.

## Core Metrics

■ **Key performance indicators.** A nonprofit adopts key performance indicators to determine how it will measure what it intends to do. Key performance indicators will vary depending on the nonprofit, but they may include performance metrics for programs, development, and productivity. These metrics provide a basis for holding individuals and teams accountable, which in turn leads to greater attention to addressing threats before they become crises and developing opportunities that minimize waste and improve performance.

- **Key risk indicators.** An organization adopts key risk indicators when it decides what events might trigger the need for countermeasures within a given function.

## Smooth Sailing Documents

- **Executive succession/transition plan.** Executive succession and transition inevitably occur in every organization. By adopting a plan, an organization reduces the likelihood of having to confront a succession issue without forethought.
- **Business continuity plan.** An organization needs to have a basic, robust plan for what to do in the event of natural disasters and other business interruptions.
- **Crisis communication plan.** A nonprofit adopts a crisis communication plan to guide the organization when it faces some adverse event. The risk management value of such a plan is manifest; it is harder to confront a crisis in the moment without forethought about how the organization intends to handle communications in such circumstances.

## Feedback Mechanisms and Records

- **Customer feedback mechanisms.** This book has emphasized that operations should always be addressed from the perspective of the customer. Customer feedback mechanisms enable organizations to gather important information from the people they serve, creating an early warning mechanism for potential threats and an identification process for potential opportunities.
- **Employee feedback mechanisms.** An organization that adopts employee feedback mechanisms (such as a suggestion box, regular inquiry during management check-in meetings, or the like) opens the potential flow of information about threats and opportunities.

- **Complaint log.** A complaint log permits stakeholders to record perceived problems so that an organization can respond appropriately.
- **Incident log.** An incident log gathers information about accidents and complaints. This provides a record for insurance, litigation, and review and follow-up.

### IT Safeguards

- **Periodic IT check-up.** Nonprofits tend to underspend on information technology. A periodic IT check-up from an outside vendor can identify threats and opportunities that nonprofit personnel have not noticed.
- **Data security backup and recovery plan.** A nonprofit needs to protect its data and provide ways to restore operations in the event of some data failure.

## Insurance

This book has emphasized that insurance is only one aspect of risk management; nevertheless, it is an important element. Directors and officers liability insurance, general liability insurance, errors and omissions insurance, and other forms of insurance reduce the magnitude of impact if a covered event happens.

# APPENDIX

# 5

# A Simple Compliance Checklist

UNFORTUNATELY, STORIES ABOUND of nonprofits that commit employment law violations, allow impermissible conflicts of interest, or violate fundraising law. Every time one of these reports surfaces, the nonprofit sector suffers another black eye, and public confidence erodes.

Most of these issues could have been avoided by proper nonprofit compliance.

But many nonprofit leaders continue to ask, "What is nonprofit compliance? What areas of my organization does it affect? How can I ensure compliance with a minimum of distraction and expense?" This appendix answers those questions.

## Definition of Nonprofit Compliance

Nonprofit compliance is the process of providing reasonable assurance that your organization obeys applicable laws, contracts, and commitments. As the *Standards for Excellence* put it, "Nonprofits must be aware of and comply with all federal, state, and local laws."[1] As a result, they "should periodically conduct an internal review of the organization's compliance with known existing legal, regulatory, and financial reporting requirements, and should provide a summary of the results to the Board of Directors."[2]

The Standards' compliance provision is correct, but it may not go far enough. In addition to legal, regulatory, and financial reporting requirements, a nonprofit organization should account for obligations it has made to other organizations and stakeholders. This may include funders, staff, clients, and volunteers.

## Nonprofit Compliance Checklist

Many resources are available to help nonprofits identify areas of potential compliance requirements. This book suggests the following items:

- **Nonprofit corporate requirements,** including business licenses, annual reports, and registered agent requirements
- **Nonprofit fundraising requirements,** including solicitation registration, disclosure statements, and annual reporting
- **Nonprofit operational requirements,** including having current bylaws, complying with those bylaws, ensuring board members comply with fiduciary duties, regular board meetings, and other issues
- **Nonprofit accounting requirements,** including tax-exempt status, filing of IRS form 990, documenting income from unrelated business activity, federal and state grant requirements, and accurate books and records
- **Proper classification of employees,** including filings relating to employees and contractors
- **Nonprofit record-keeping requirements**, including required state and federal records, what records need to be available to the public, copies of federal and state tax returns for three years, and a records retention process

- **Private grant compliance.** Nonprofits must comply with reporting and other obligations in any private grant received.
- **Restricted funds compliance.** If your nonprofit receives restricted donations, it must comply with those restrictions.
- **Workforce health and safety.** Federal and state health and safety regulations likely apply to your nonprofit. SafetyCulture .com provides an excellent checklist on its website, and ProBonoPartner.org has a useful OSHA guide for nonprofits on its site.
- **Data security and privacy.** Any nonprofit that conducts e-commerce on its website (such as donations or event registrations), stores or transfers personally identifiable information, or collects electronic information about the habits of its donors, stakeholders, or clients must also account for data security and privacy requirements.
- **Employment compliance, including nondiscrimination, harassment, and whistleblower issues.** Nonprofits often make employment mistakes. As a result, it is important for nonprofits to be aware of employment issues.
- **Local and state zoning and licensure compliance.** Certain activities require permits, and many services require licensure.
- **Compliance with self-imposed requirements.** If your organization has adopted protocols or procedures to address volunteers, clients, or others, you should provide reasonable assurance that you are in fact meeting those obligations.

## What Should You Do Now?

The previous list may give you heartburn. It can feel overwhelming. Nonprofits do so much good in the world: why did they have to comply with all these rules? How does compliance leave time to perform services for those in need?

The emotion is understandable, but the answer is clear. Nonprofits have an obligation to abide by the rules, just like anyone else. In fact, compliance is more important in the nonprofit sector. Nonprofits perform critical functions in our society. They cannot afford costly, unforced errors.

Furthermore, with slow and steady work, you can ensure smooth compliance in your organization without undue burden. The approach to compliance is analogous to the Lean Risk Management methodology described in this book. Here is a nine-step approach:

1. **Have your board set the tone at the top.** One of the most important functions of a board of directors is to set the tone at the top. Make sure that your board emphasizes the priority of compliance measures.

2. **Assess your status.** Use the previous list and linked nonprofit resources to identify what you need to comply with. Be aware that in this first step you will find areas of noncompliance. No organization is perfect, and any organization that has not evaluated its compliance status in the past is going to find issues. As a result, prepare to find issues in need of attention.

3. **Delegate and ask people to be devil's advocates.** Do not try to do this all on your own. Instead, create a task force and assign staff members to look at different areas. Ask them to err on the side of reporting. In this initial stage, you want to identify potential issues, not sweep them under the rug.

4. **Prioritize and perform ongoing remediation.** If you have a nonprofit risk management process, add problem areas to your risk register and prioritize relative to other issues. If you do not, prioritize in the following manner:
   o Issues creating potential risks and legal liability
   o Health and safety of employees and clients
   o Violations of policies or ethical practices
   o Ambiguity about legal obligations
   o Everything else

5. **Name, claim, record, and celebrate successes.** As you confirm compliance in an area or take steps to remediate, celebrate

those wins. This will create ongoing momentum and provide the staff and board with assurance that the organization intends to pay attention to its obligations.

6. **Outsource when you can do that cost-effectively.** Your accountant may be able to cover many compliance issues. Your attorney may be able to address others. Organizations exist that can help with fundraising registration compliance. Do not do it on your own when someone else can do it better and less expensively.

7. **Provide targeted training.** As you work through compliance, identify risks and areas where your staff needs guidance. Get them the training they need.

8. **Document and systematize.** Capture your compliance requirements in simple protocols that people can follow to avoid compliance challenges down the road.

9. **Do not just talk—do.** As nonprofit instructor Nancy Bacon notes, "You don't get compliance by" simply "talking about compliance."[3]

# Sources and Methodology

AN EARLY VERSION of this book sought to footnote every page. The lawyer in me craves citations. In this published version, however, I adopted a different approach. I have referenced important items along the way. The basis of the Lean Risk Management methodology, however, are *Enterprise Risk Management—Integrated Framework* and ISO 31000.

In developing the Lean Risk Management approach, I also have relied on nearly 30 years of helping nonprofits. In addition, I have relied on Risk Alternatives' proprietary survey data from hundreds of nonprofits around the United States.

In the following sections I provide materials on risk management, Lean management, systems thinking, and design thinking, as well as a bibliography of all materials cited in this book.

## Books on Risk and Risk Management

Fungston, Frederick, and Stephen Wagner. *Surviving and Thriving in Uncertainty: Creating the Risk Intelligent Enterprise*. New York, NY: Wiley, 2010.

Herman, Melanie L. *Ready or Not: A Risk Management Guide for Nonprofit Executives*, 2nd ed. Leesburg, VA: Nonprofit Risk Management Center, 2011.

Herman, Melanie L., George L. Head, Peggy M. Jackson, and Toni E. Fogarty. *Managing Risk in Nonprofit Organizations: A Comprehensive Guide*. New York, NY: Wiley, 2004.

Hubbard, Douglas. *The Failure of Risk Management: Why It's Broken and How to Fix It*. New York, NY: Wiley, 2009.

Marks, Norman, and Melanie L. Herman. *World-Class Risk Management for Nonprofits*. Leesburg, VA: Nonprofit Risk Management Center, 2019.

Ropeik, David, and George Gray. *Risk: A Practical Guide for Deciding What's Really Safe and What's Really Dangerous in the World Around You*. Boston, MA: Mariner Books, 2002.

Segal, Sim. *The Corporate Value of Enterprise Risk Management: The Next Step in Business Management*. New York, NY: Wiley, 2011.

Taleb, Nassim Nicholas. *Fooled by Randomness: The Hidden Role of Chance in Life and in the Markets*. New York, NY: Random House, 2004.

Taleb, Nassim Nicholas. *The Black Swan: The Impact of the Highly Improbable*. New York, NY: Random House Publishing Group, 2007.

Taleb, Nassim Nicholas. *Antifragile: Things That Gain from Disorder*. New York, NY: Random House, 2012.

Viscott, David. *Risking*. New York, NY: Pocket Books, 1977.

## Books on Lean Management

Chase, Richard B., and Douglas M. Stewart. *Mistake-Proofing: Designing Errors Out*. New York, NY: Productivity Press, 2002.

DeGrandis, Dominica. *Making Work Visible: Exposing Time Theft to Optimize Work & Flow*. Portland, OR: IT Revolution Press, 2017.

Deming, W. Edwards. *Out of the Crisis*. Cambridge, MA: MIT Center for Advanced Engineering Study, 1986.

George, Michael. *Lean Six Sigma for Service: How to Use Lean Speed and Six Sigma Quality to Improve Services and Transactions*. New York, NY: McGraw-Hill, 2003.

George, Michael, David Rowlands, Mark Price, and John Maxey. *The Lean Six Sigma Pocket Toolbook: A Quick Reference Guide to 100 Tools for Improving Quality and Speed*. New York, NY: McGraw-Hill, 2005.

Keyte, Beau, and Drew Lochner. *The Complete Lean Enterprise: Value Stream Mapping for Office and Services.* New York, NY: Productivity Press, 2004.

Langley, Gerald, Kevin Nolan, Thomas Nolan, Clifford Norman, and Lloyd Provost. *The Improvement Guide: A Practical Approach to Enhancing Organizational Performance.* San Francisco, CA: Jossey-Bass, 1996.

Liker, Jeffrey K., and Gary Convis. *The Toyota Way to Lean Leadership: Achieving and Sustaining Excellence Through Leadership Development.* New York, NY: McGraw-Hill, 2012.

Liker, Jeffrey K., and David Meier. *The Toyota Way Fieldbook.* New York, NY: McGraw-Hill, 2006.

Liker, Jeffrey K., and Karyn Ross. *The Toyota Way to Service Excellence: Lean Transformation in Service Organizations.* New York, NY: McGraw-Hill, 2017.

Martin, Karen. *Clarity First: How Smart Leaders and Organizations Achieve Outstanding Performance.* New York, NY: McGraw-Hill, 2018.

Martin, Karen, and Mike Osterling. *Value Stream Mapping: How to Visualize Work and Align Leadership for Organizational Transformation.* New York, NY: McGraw-Hill, 2013.

Miller, Jon, Mike Wroblewski, and Jaime Villafuerte. *Creating a Kaizen Culture: Align the Organization, Achieve Breakthrough Results, and Sustain the Gains.* New York, NY: McGraw-Hill, 2014.

Modig, Niklas, and Par Ahlstrom. *This Is Lean: Resolving the Paradox.* Stockholm, Sweden: Rheologica Publishing, 2017.

Pryor, Robert. *Lean Selling: Slash Your Sales Cycle and Drive Profitable, Predictable Revenue Growth.* Bloomington, IN: AuthorHouse, 2014.

Ptacek, Rob, Todd Sperl, and Jayant Trewn. *The Practical Lean Six Sigma Pocket Guide: Using the A3 and Lean Thinking to Improve Operational Performance in ANY Industry, Any Time!* Chelsea, MI: MCS Media, 2013.

Ptacek, Rob, and Jaideep Motwani. *Lean Six Sigma for Service—Pursuing Perfect Service.* Chelsea, MI: MCS Media, 2011.

Rother, Mike. *Toyota Kata: Managing People for Improvement, Adaptiveness, and Superior Results.* New York, NY: McGraw-Hill, 2010.

Venegas, Carlos. *Flow in the Office: Implementing and Sustaining Lean Improvements.* New York, NY: Productivity Press, 2007.

Womack, James, and Daniel T. Jones. *Lean Solutions*. New York, NY: Free Press, 2005.

Womack, James, Daniel Jones, and Daniel Roos. *The Machine That Changed the World: The Story of Lean Production*. New York, NY: Harper Perennial, 1990.

## Books on Systems Thinking

Matthews, Donella. *Thinking in Systems*. Chelsea, VT: Chelsea Green Publishing, 2008.

Senge, Peter. *The Fifth Discipline*. New York, NY: Currency, 1990.

Senge, Peter, Richard Ross, Bryan Smith, Charlotte Roberts, and Art Kleiner. *The Fifth Discipline Fieldbook: Strategies and Tools for Building a Learning Organization*. New York, NY: Currency, 1994.

## Books on Design Thinking

Brown, Tim. *Change by Design: How Design Thinking Transforms Organizations and Inspires Innovation*, rev. ed. New York, NY: Harper Business, 2019.

Harvard Business Review. *HBR's 10 Must Reads on Design Thinking*. Cambridge, MA: Harvard Business Review Press, 2020.

## Other Cited Materials

Abraham, Jay. *Getting Everything You Can Out of All You've Got: 21 Ways You Can Out-Think, Out-Perform, and Out-Earn the Competition*. New York, NY: St. Martin's Griffin, 2001.

"Are You Familiar with Wrongdoing Among Nonprofit Groups?" *New York Times*, March 21, 2022. https://www.nytimes.com/2022/03/21/reader-center/nonprofit-wrongdoing.html.

Bacon, Nancy. "You Don't Get Compliance by Talking About Compliance." *NancyBacon.com* (blog), October 5, 2021. https://nancybacon.com/you-dont-get-compliance-by-talking-about-compliance/.

Behesti, Naz. "10 Timely Statistics About the Connection Between Employee Engagement and Wellness." *Forbes*, January 16, 2019. https://www.forbes.com/sites/nazbeheshti/2019/01/16/10-timely-statistics-about-the-connection-between-employee-engagement-and-wellness/?sh=cbe817a22a03.

Bell, Megan E., and Tomer J. Inbar. "Cybersecurity & Nonprofits: A Matter of Time?" *Data Security Law Blog* (blog), November 18, 2015. https://www.pbwt.com/data-security-law-blog/cybersecurity-nonprofits-a-matter-of-time.

Bloom, Paul N., and J. Gregory Dees. "Cultivate Your Ecosystem." *Stanford Social Innovation Review*, Winter 2008. https://ssir.org/articles/entry/cultivate_your_ecosystem.

BoardSource. *The Nonprofit Board Answer Book: A Practical Guide for Board Members and Chief Executives*. San Francisco, CA: Jossey-Bass, 2011.

Bolton, Peter. "Nonprofit Employers Don't Meet Workers' Needs for Job Satisfaction, Surveys Find." *The Chronicle of Philanthropy* (blog), October 24, 2011. https://www.philanthropy.com/article/nonprofit-employers-dont-meet-workers-needs-for-job-satisfaction-surveys-find/.

Buteau, Ellie, Andrea Brock, and Mark Chaffin. *Nonprofit Challenges: What Foundations Can Do*. Cambridge, MA: Center for Effective Philanthropy, 2013. http://cep.org/wp-content/uploads/2016/08/NonprofitChallenges.pdf.

The Case Foundation. "The Pros and Cons of Working in the Nonprofit Sector." *The Case Foundation* (blog), February 17, 2011. https://casefoundation.org/blog/pros-and-cons-working-nonprofit-sector/.

Cohen, Rick. "Nonprofit Salaries: Achieving Parity with the Private Sector." *Nonprofit Quarterly*, June 21, 2010. https://nonprofitquarterly.org/nonprofit-salaries-achieving-parity-with-the-private-sector/.

Collins, Jim. *Good to Great: Why Some Companies Make the Leap . . . and Others Don't*. New York, NY: HarperBusiness, 2001.

Cornelius, Marla, and Patrick Corvington. "Nonprofit Workforce Dynamics." In Lester M. Salamon (ed.), *The State of Nonprofit America*, 2nd ed. Washington, DC: Brookings Institution Press, 2012, 639–656.

Covey, Stephen. *The Seven Habits of Highly Effective People*. New York, NY: Simon & Schuster, 1990.

Criminal Justice Caucus at the Columbia School of Social Work. "Review of 'No One Wants to Work with Me: Working with Difficult Populations.'" *Criminal Justice Caucus* (blog), April 17, 2012. https://criminaljusticecaucus.wordpress.com/2012/04/17/review-of-no-one-wants-to-work-with-me-working-with-difficult-populations-workshop/.

District of Columbia Bar. *A Nonprofit's Guide to Risk Management and Insurance.* Washington, DC: Public Counsel and DC Bar Pro Bono Program, 2013. https://www.lawhelp.org/files/7C92C43F-9283-A7E0-5931-E57134E903FB/attachments/BC5C891A-81F7-40BA-924A-7C0DE04F0E10/risk-management-manual(1).pdf.

Drucker, Peter. *People and Performance: The Best of Peter Drucker on Management.* Cambridge, MA: Harvard Business Review Press, 1977.

Dubb, Steve. "New York City Alleges Homeless Shelter Nonprofit Engaged in Massive Fraud." *Nonprofit Quarterly*, February 4, 2020. https://nonprofitquarterly.org/new-york-city-alleges-homeless-shelter-nonprofit-engaged-in-massive-fraud/#:~:text=As%20Nikita%20Stewart%20details%20in,against%20the%20nonprofit%20on%20Wednesday.%E2%80%9D.

Francis, Angela, and Jennifer Talansky. *Small Nonprofits Solving Big Problems.* New York, NY: Nonprofit Finance Fund, 2012. https://nff.org/report/small-nonprofits-solving-big-problems.

Garry, Joan. *Joan Garry's Guide to Nonprofit Leadership: Because the World Is Counting on You,* 2nd ed. New York, NY: Wiley, 2020.

Garvey, David. "Nonprofit Sector: Workforce Education Needs and Opportunities." *Continuing Higher Education Review* 73, Fall 2009: 114–124. https://files.eric.ed.gov/fulltext/EJ903456.pdf.

Gawande, Atul. *The Checklist Manifesto: How to Get Things Right.* London, UK: Picador, 2010.

Gibbons-Neff, Thomas. "Wounded Warrior Project Executives Fired Amid Controversy." *Washington Post*, March 10, 2016. https://www.washingtonpost.com/news/checkpoint/wp/2016/03/10/report-wounded-warrior-project-executives-fired-amid-controversy/.

Goggins Gregory, Ann, and Don Howard. "The Nonprofit Starvation Cycle." *Stanford Social Innovation Review*, Fall 2009. https://ssir.org/articles/entry/the_nonprofit_starvation_cycle.

Gray, Jeff. "Toronto Goodwill Moving Forward with Bankruptcy, CEO to Step Down." *Globe and Mail*, February 29, 2016. https://www.theglobeandmail.com/news/national/efforts-to-revive-goodwill-have-failed-says-ceo/article28947165/.

Herzlinger, Regina E. "Effective Oversight." *Harvard Business Review*, July/August 1994: 93–106.

The Hewlett Foundation. *The Nonprofit Marketplace: Bridging the Information Gap in Philanthropy*, 2008. https://hewlett.org/wp-content/uploads/2016/08/whitepaper.pdf.

Hillman, Robert A. *Principles of Contract Law*. St. Paul, MN: Thomson West, 2004.

Hiscox USA. *The 2015 Hiscox Embezzlement Watchlist*. https://www.hiscox.com/documents/brokers/2015%20Hiscox%20Embezzlement%20Watchlist.pdf.

Hopper, Joe. "How to Label Your 10-Point Scale." *Versta Research* (blog), November 2014. https://verstaresearch.com/blog/how-to-label-your-10-point-scale/.

Hubbard, Douglas. *How to Measure Anything: Finding the Value of Intangibles in Business*. New York, NY: Wiley, 2010.

Human Services Corporation of New York. *New York Nonprofits in the Aftermath of FEGS: A Call to Action*. New York, NY: Human Services Corporation of New York, 2016. https://philanthropynewyork.org/sites/default/files/resources/HSCCommissionReport.pdf.

Independent Sector. *Independent Sector Principles for Good Governance and Ethical Practice*. Washington, DC: Independent Sector, 2015. https://independentsector.org/wp-content/uploads/2016/11/Principles2018-Final-Web.pdf.

Institute for Public Relations. *Organizational Clarity: The Case for Workforce Alignment & Belief*. May 16, 2016. https://instituteforpr.org/wp-content/uploads/Organizational-Clarity-White-Paper-05–06–16-Final-Online.pdf.

Jones, Harriet E., and Dani L. Long. *Principles of Insurance: Life, Health, and Annuities*, 2nd ed. Atlanta, GA: Life Office Management Association, 1999.

Jonker, Kim, and William F. Meehan III. "Fundamentals, Not Fads." *Stanford Social Innovation Review*, Spring 2014. https://ssir.org/articles/entry/fundamentals_not_fads#:~:text=Fundamentals%2C%20Not%20Fads,%2C%20Funding%2C%20Leadership%2C%20etc.

Kanter, Beth, and Allison Fine. *The Smart Nonprofit: Staying Human-Centered in an Automated World*. New York, NY: Wiley, 2022.

Kearns, Kevin P. "Accountability in the Nonprofit Sector." In Lester M. Salamon (ed.), *The State of Nonprofit America*, 2nd ed. Washington, DC: Brookings Institution Press, 2012, 587–615.

Klein, Gary, "Performing a Project Premortem." *Harvard Business Review*, September, 2007. https://hbr.org/2007/09/performing-a-project-premortem.

Korngold, Alice. "Nonprofit Boards: On Saying No to Problem Board Members." *Fast Company* (blog), March 18, 2011. https://www.fastcompany.com/1739927/nonprofit-boards-saying-no-problem-board-members.

Krafcik, John. "Triumph of the Lean Production System." *Sloan Management Review*, Fall 1988. https://edisciplinas.usp.br/pluginfile.php/5373958/mod_resource/content/4/krafcik_TEXTO_INTEGRAL.pdf.

Landles-Cobb, Libbie, Kirk Kramer, and Katie Smith Milway. "The Nonprofit Leadership Development Deficit." *Stanford Social Innovation Review*, October 22, 2015. https://ssir.org/articles/entry/the_nonprofit_leadership_development_deficit.

Larcker, David, Nicholas Donatiello, Bill Meehan, and Brian Tayan. *2015 Survey on Board of Directors of Nonprofit Organizations*. Stanford, CA: Stanford Graduate School of Business, 1996. https://www.gsb.stanford.edu/sites/default/files/publication-pdf/cgri-survey-nonprofit-board-directors-2015.pdf.

Leahy, Robert. *Cognitive Therapy Techniques: A Practitioner's Guide*. New York, NY: Guilford Press, 2003.

MacKay, Jory. "The Everything Is Important Paradox: 9 Practical Methods for How to Prioritize Your Work (and Time)." *RescueTime* (blog), May 5, 2020. https://blog.rescuetime.com/how-to-prioritize/.

Manzo, Peter. "The Real Salary Scandal." *Stanford Social Innovation Review*, Winter 2004. https://ssir.org/articles/entry/the_real_salary_scandal.

McCambridge, Ruth. "The FEGS Autopsy: Bad Nonprofit Business in a Tough Operating Environment." *Nonprofit Quarterly*, February 26, 2016. https://nonprofitquarterly.org/the-fegs-autopsy-a-case-of-bad-nonprofit-business-in-a-tough-operating-environment/.

McKeown, Greg. *Essentialism: The Disciplined Pursuit of Less*. New York, NY: Crown, 2020.

Milway, Katie Smith, Maria Orozco, and Christina Botero. "Why Nonprofit Mergers Continue to Lag." *Stanford Social Innovation Review*, Spring 2014. https://ssir.org/articles/entry/why_nonprofit_mergers_continue_to_lag.

Minnesota Council of Nonprofits. *Principles & Practices for Nonprofit Excellence*. St. Paul, MN: Minnesota Council of Nonprofits, 2014. https://www.minnesotanonprofits.org/docs/default-source/publications/principles-and-practices—full-publication.pdf?sfvrsn=93531894_4.

Mintz, Joshua. "Risky Business: Why All Nonprofits Should Periodically Assess Their Risk." *Nonprofit Quarterly*, May 8, 2012. https://nonprofitquarterly.org/risky-business-why-all-nonprofits-should-periodically-assess-their-risk/.

Nonprofit Finance Fund. *State of the Nonprofit Sector 2015 Survey*. New York, NY: Nonprofit Finance Fund, 2015. https://nff.org/report/2015-state-sector-survey-brochure.

Nonprofit Times, "Job Satisfaction Up, Majority Still Not Thrilled." *Nonprofit Times*, September 9, 2015. http://www.thenonprofittimes.com/news-articles/job-satisfaction-up-majority-still-not-thrilled/.

Opportunity Knocks. *Engaging the Nonprofit Workforce: Mission, Management and Emotion*, 2011. https://www.gcn.org/sites/default/files/ctools/OK_Engaging_the_Nonprofit_Workforce_Report.pdf.

Princeton Survey Research Associates. *Health of the Nonprofit, For-Profit, and Public Service Sectors*, February 15, 2002. https://www.brookings.edu/wp-content/uploads/2016/06/NonprofitTopline.pdf.

Salamon, Lester M. "The Resilient Sector: The Future of Nonprofit America." In Lester M. Salamon (ed.), *The State of Nonprofit America*, 2nd ed. Washington, DC: Brookings Institution Press, 2012, 3–86.

Salls, Manda. "Why Nonprofits Have a Board Problem." *Harvard Business School Working Knowledge* (blog), April 4, 2005. https://hbswk.hbs.edu/archive/why-nonprofits-have-a-board-problem.

Savage, Sam. *The Flaw of Averages: Why We Underestimate Risk in the Face of Uncertainty*. New York, NY: Wiley, 2012.

Schmidt, Elizabeth. "Rediagnosing 'Founder's Syndrome': Moving Beyond Stereotypes to Improve Nonprofit Performance." *Nonprofit Quarterly*, July 1, 2013. https://nonprofitquarterly.org/rediagnosing-founder-s-syndrome-moving-beyond-stereotypes-to-improve-nonprofit-performance/.

Scott, Susan. *Fierce Conversations: Achieving Success at Work and in Life One Conversation at a Time*. New York, NY: Berkley Publishing, 2004.

Smith, Barry D., and Eric A. Wiening, *How Insurance Works*, 2nd ed. Malvern, PA: American Institute for Chartered Property Casualty Underwriters/Insurance Institute of America, 1994.

*Standards for Excellence®: An Ethics and Accountability Code for the Nonprofit Sector, Finance and Operations*. Baltimore, MD: Maryland Nonprofits, 2014.

Stephens, Joe, and Mary Pat Flaherty. "Inside the Hidden World of Thefts, Scams, and Phantom Purchases at the Nation's Nonprofits." *Washington Post*, October 26, 2013. https://www.washingtonpost.com/investigations/inside-the-hidden-world-of-thefts-scams-and-phantom-purchases-at-the-nations-nonprofits/2013/10/26/825a82ca-0c26-11e3-9941-6711ed662e71_story.html.

Tigar, Lindsay. "5 Ways Anxiety Can Sabotage Your Work Performance (and How to Keep It at Bay)." *Yahoo!Life* (blog), March 31, 2021. https://www.yahoo.com/lifestyle/5-ways-anxiety-sabotage-performance-195818640.html.

Utah Food Bank. *Utah Food Bank Responds to Possible Data Security Incident*. Utah Food Bank Press Release, Aug. 31, 2015. https://www.utahfoodbank.org/wp-content/uploads/2017/03/Utah-Food-Bank-Responds-to-Possible-Data-Security-Incident.pdf.

Wickman, Geno. *Traction: Get a Grip on Your Business*. Dallas, TX: BenBella, 2011.

Yin, Lijun, Ruzhen Mao, and Zijun Ke. "Charity Misconduct on Public Health Issues Impairs Willingness to Offer Help." *International Journal of Environmental Research and Public Health*, December, 2021. https://www.ncbi.nlm.nih.gov/pmc/articles/PMC8700860/#:~:text=Results%20showed%20that%20charity%20misconduct,(Study%201%20and%202).

Young, Dennis R., Lester M. Salamon, and Mary Clark Grinsfelder. "Commercialization, Social Ventures, and For-Profit Competition." In Lester M. Salamon (ed.), *The State of Nonprofit America*, 2nd ed. Washington, DC: Brookings Institution Press, 2012, 521–548.

# Notes

## Chapter 1

1. Lester M. Salamon, "The Resilient Sector: The Future of Nonprofit America," in Lester M. Salamon (ed.), *The State of Nonprofit America*, 2nd ed. (Washington, DC: Brookings Institution Press, 2012), 12.
2. *Independent Sector Principles for Good Governance and Ethical Practice* (Washington, DC: Independent Sector, 2015) (https://independentsector.org/wp-content/uploads/2016/11/Principles2018-Final-Web.pdf), 16.
3. Ibid.
4. *Standards for Excellence®: An Ethics and Accountability Code for the Nonprofit Sector* (Baltimore, MD: Maryland Nonprofits, 2014) (https://standardsforexcellence.org/Home-2/code).
5. Minnesota Council of Nonprofits, *Principles & Practices for Nonprofit Excellence* (St. Paul, MN: Minnesota Council of Nonprofits, 2014) (https://www.minnesotanonprofits.org/docs/default-source/publications/principles-and-practices—full-publication.pdf?sfvrsn=93531894_4), 18.
6. District of Columbia Bar, *A Nonprofit's Guide to Risk Management and Insurance* (Washington, DC: Public Counsel and DC Bar Pro Bono Program, 2013) (https://www.lawhelp.org/files/7C92C43F-9283-A7E0–5931-E57134E903FB/attachments/BC5C891A-81F7–40BA-924A-7C0DE04F0E10/risk-management-manual(1).pdf), 1.

7. Human Services Corporation of New York, *New York Nonprofits in the Aftermath of FEGS: A Call to Action* (New York, NY: Human Services Corporation of New York, 2016) (https://philanthropynewyork .org/sites/default/files/resources/HSCCommissionReport.pdf), 26.

8. Proprietary research held by Risk Alternatives LLC. Data current through May 2022. Percentages exceed 100% due to rounding.

9. Sim Segal, *The Corporate Value of Enterprise Risk Management: The Next Step in Business Management* (New York, NY: Wiley, 2011), 4–5.

10. Committee of Sponsoring Organizations of the Treadway Commission, *Enterprise Risk Management—Integrated Framework* (2004). https://www.coso.org/Shared%20Documents/2017-COSO-ERM-Integrating-with-Strategy-and-Performance-Executive-Summary.pdf

11. International Organization for Standardization, ISO 31000 (Geneva, Switzerland: International Organization for Standardization, 2009).

12. Securities Exchange Commission, "SEC Approves Enhanced Disclosure About Risk, Compensation and Corporate Governance" (Washington, DC: SEC Release 2009–268, December 16, 2009).

13. Thomas Gibbons-Neff, "Wounded Warrior Project Executives Fired Amid Controversy," *Washington Post* (March 10, 2016) (https://www .washingtonpost.com/news/checkpoint/wp/2016/03/10/report-wounded-warrior-project-executives-fired-amid-controversy/).

14. Jeff Gray, "Toronto Goodwill Moving Forward with Bankruptcy, CEO to Step Down," *Globe and Mail* (February 29, 2016) (https://www .theglobeandmail.com/news/national/efforts-to-revive-goodwill-have-failed-says-ceo/article28947165/).

15. Ruth McCambridge, "The FEGS Autopsy: Bad Nonprofit Business in a Tough Operating Environment," *Nonprofit Quarterly* (February 26, 2016) (https://nonprofitquarterly.org/the-fegs-autopsy-a-case-of-bad-nonprofit-business-in-a-tough-operating-environment/).

16. Steve Dubb, "New York City Alleges Homeless Shelter Nonprofit Engaged in Massive Fraud," *Nonprofit Quarterly* (February 4, 2020) (https://nonprofitquarterly.org/new-york-city-alleges-homeless-shelter-nonprofit-engaged-in-massive-fraud/#:~:text=As%20 Nikita%20Stewart%20details%20in,against%20the%20nonprofit% 20on%20Wednesday.%E2%80%9D).

17. Hiscox USA, *The 2015 Hiscox Embezzlement Watchlist* (2015) (https://www.hiscox.com/documents/brokers/2015%20Hiscox%20Embezzlement%20Watchlist.pdf).

18. Joe Stephens and Mary Pat Flaherty, "Inside the Hidden World of Thefts, Scams, and Phantom Purchases at the Nation's Nonprofits" *Washington Post* (October 26, 2013) (https://www.washingtonpost.com/investigations/inside-the-hidden-world-of-thefts-scams-and-phantom-purchases-at-the-nations-nonprofits/2013/10/26/825a82ca-0c26–11e3–9941–6711ed662e71_story.html).

19. Utah Food Bank, *Utah Food Bank Responds to Possible Data Security Incident* (Utah Food Bank Press Release August 31, 2015) (https://www.utahfoodbank.org/wp-content/uploads/2017/03/Utah-Food-Bank-Responds-to-Possible-Data-Security-Incident.pdf).

20. Megan E. Bell and Tomer J. Inbar, "Cybersecurity & Nonprofits: A Matter of Time?" *Data Security Law Blog* (blog) (November 18, 2015) (https://www.pbwt.com/data-security-law-blog/cybersecurity-nonprofits-a-matter-of-time).

21. Robert Leahy, *Cognitive Therapy Techniques: A Practitioner's Guide* (New York, NY: Guilford Press, 2003), 102.

22. Joan Garry, *Joan Garry's Guide to Nonprofit Leadership: Because the World Is Counting on You* (New York, NY: Wiley, 2020), xx.

23. "Are You Familiar with Wrongdoing Among Nonprofit Groups?" *New York Times* (March 21, 2022) (https://www.nytimes.com/2022/03/21/reader-center/nonprofit-wrongdoing.html).

24. Lijun Yin, Ruzhen Mao, and Zijun Ke, "Charity Misconduct on Public Health Issues Impairs Willingness to Offer Help," *International Journal of Environmental Research and Public Health* (December 2021) (https://www.ncbi.nlm.nih.gov/pmc/articles/PMC8700860/#:~:text=Results%20showed%20that%20charity%20misconduct,(Study%201%20and%202).

25. Beth Kanter and Allison Fine, *The Smart Nonprofit: Staying Human-Centered in an Automated World* (New York, NY: Wiley, 2022).

26. Lindsey Tigar, "5 Ways Anxiety Can Sabotage Your Work Performance (and How to Keep It at Bay)" *Yahoo!Life* (blog) (March 31, 2021) (https://www.yahoo.com/lifestyle/5-ways-anxiety-sabotage-performance-195818640.html).

27. Institute for Public Relations, *Organizational Clarity: The Case for Workforce Alignment & Belief* (May 16, 2016) (https://instituteforpr. org/wp-content/uploads/Organizational-Clarity-White-Paper-05–06–16-Final-Online.pdf).
28. Naz Behesti, "10 Timely Statistics About the Connection Between Employee Engagement and Wellness," *Forbes* (January 16, 2019) (https://www.forbes.com/sites/nazbeheshti/2019/01/16/10-timely-statistics-about-the-connection-between-employee-engagement-and-wellness/?sh=cbe817a22a03).

## Chapter 2

1. Douglas Hubbard, *The Failure of Risk Management: Why It's Broken and How to Fix It* (New York, NY: Wiley, 2009), 80.
2. Sim Segal, *The Corporate Value of Enterprise Risk Management: The Next Step in Business Management* (New York, NY: Wiley, 2011), 19.
3. Nassim Nicholas Taleb, *The Black Swan: The Impact of the Highly Improbable* (New York, NY: Random House Publishing Group, 2007).
4. James Womack, Daniel Jones, and Daniel Roos, *The Machine That Changed the World: The Story of Lean Production* (New York, NY: Harper Perennial, 1991).
5. John Krafcik, "Triumph of the Lean Production System," *Sloan Management Review* (Fall 1988) (https://edisciplinas.usp.br/pluginfile. php/5373958/mod_resource/content/4/krafcik_TEXTO_ INTEGRAL.pdf).
6. Michael L. George, *Lean Six Sigma for Service: How to Use Lean Speed and Six Sigma Quality to Improve Services and Transactions* (New York, NY: McGraw-Hill, 2003).
7. Jon Miller, Mike Wroblewski, and Jaime Villafuerte, *Creating a Kaizen Culture: Align the Organization, Achieve Breakthrough Results, and Sustain the Gains* (New York, NY: McGraw-Hill, 2014), xv.
8. Karen Martin and Mike Osterling, *Value Stream Mapping: How to Visualize Work and Align Leadership for Organizational Transformation* (New York, NY: McGraw-Hill, 2013).

## Part I

1. Jim Collins, *Good to Great: Why Some Companies Make the Leap . . . and Others Don't* (New York, NY: HarperBusiness, 2001).

## Chapter 3

1. Peter Drucker, *People and Performance: The Best of Peter Drucker on Management* (Cambridge, MA: Harvard Business Review Press, 1977), 33.
2. Carlos Venegas, *Flow in the Office: Implementing and Sustaining Lean Improvements* (New York, NY: Productivity Press, 2007), 10.
3. Stephen Covey, *The Seven Habits of Highly Effective People* (New York, NY: Simon & Shuster, 1990), 81–86.
4. Susan Scott, *Fierce Conversations: Achieving Success at Work and in Life One Conversation at a Time* (New York, NY: Berkley Publishing, 2004).
5. Karen Martin, *Clarity First: How Smart Leaders and Organizations Achieve Outstanding Performance* (New York, NY: McGraw-Hill, 2018).
6. Peter Senge, Richard Ross, Bryan Smith, Charlotte Roberts, and Art Kleiner, *The Fifth Discipline Fieldbook* (New York, NY: Currency, 1994).

## Part II

1. Greg McKeown, *Essentialism: The Disciplined Pursuit of Less* (New York, NY: Crown, 2014), 20.

## Chapter 4

1. Joe Hopper, "How to Label Your 10-Point Scale," *Versta Research* (blog) (Nov. 2014) (https://verstaresearch.com/blog/how-to-label-your-10-point-scale/).
2. Douglas Hubbard, *How to Measure Anything: Finding the Value of Intangibles in Business* (New York, NY: Wiley, 2010).
3. Sam Savage, *The Flaw of Averages: Why We Underestimate Risk in the Face of Uncertainty* (New York, NY: Wiley, 2012).
4. Jory MacKay, "The Everything Is Important Paradox: 9 Practical Methods for How to Prioritize Your Work (and Time)," *RescueTime* (blog) (May 5, 2020) (https://blog.rescuetime.com/how-to-prioritize/).

## Chapter 5

1. Proprietary research held by Risk Alternatives LLC.

## Part III

1. Joshua Mintz, "Risky Business: Why All Nonprofits Should Periodically Assess Their Risk," *Nonprofit Quarterly* (May 8, 2012) (https://nonprofitquarterly.org/risky-business-why-all-nonprofits-should-periodically-assess-their-risk/).

## Chapter 6

1. Carlos Venegas, *Flow in the Office: Implementing and Sustaining Lean Improvements* (New York, NY: Productivity Press, 2007), 76.
2. Jeffrey Liker and David Meier, *The Toyota Way Fieldbook* (New York, NY: McGraw-Hill, 2006), 60–61.
3. Ibid., 342–346.
4. Michael George, David Rowlands, Mark Price, and John Maxey, *The Lean Six Sigma Pocket Toolbook: A Quick Reference Guide to 100 Tools for Improving Quality and Speed* (New York, NY: McGraw-Hill, 2005), 270–273.
5. Gary Klein, "Performing a Project Premortem" *Harvard Business Review* (September 2007) (https://hbr.org/2007/09/performing-a-project-premortem).
6. George, Rowlands, Price, and Maxey, *The Lean Six Sigma Pocket Toolbook*, 146.
7. Nassim Nicholas Taleb, *Antifragile* (New York, NY: Random House, 2012), 72.
8. W. Edwards Deming, *Out of the Crisis* (Cambridge, MA: MIT Center for Advanced Engineering Study, 1986), 53.
9. Robert Pryor, *Lean Selling: Slash Your Sales Cycle and Drive Profitable, Predictable Revenue Growth* (Bloomington, IN: AuthorHouse, 2014), 87.
10. Deming, *Out of the Crisis*, 249.
11. Pryor, *Lean Selling*, 93.
12. Gino Wickman, *Traction: Get a Grip on Your Business* (Dallas, TX: BenBella, 2011), 154.
13. Karen Martin and Mike Osterling, *Value Stream Mapping: How to Visualize Work and Align Leadership for Organizational Transformation* (New York, NY: McGraw-Hill, 2013), 52.
14. Rob Ptacek, Todd Sperl, and Jayant Trewn, *The Practical Lean Six Sigma Pocket Guide: Using the A3 and Lean Thinking to Improve*

*Operational Performance in ANY Industry, ANY Time* (Chelsea, MI: MCS Media 2013).

15. Atul Gawande, *The Checklist Manifesto: How to Get Things Right* (London, UK: Picador, 2010), 120.

16. Liker and Meier, *The Toyota Way Fieldbook*, 186.

17. Deming, *Out of the Crisis*, 28.

18. Jay Abraham, *Getting Everything You Can Out of All You've Got: 21 Ways You Can Out-Think, Out-Perform, and Out-Earn the Competition* (New York, NY: St. Martin's Griffin, 2001), 151.

19. Gerald Langley, Kevin Nolan, Thomas Nolan, Clifford Norman, and Lloyd Provost, *The Improvement Guide: A Practical Approach to Enhancing Organizational Performance* (San Francisco, CA: Jossey-Bass, 1996), 24.

20. Ibid., 25.

21. Tim Brown, *Change by Design: How Design Thinking Transforms Organizations and Inspires Innovation*, rev. ed. (New York, NY: Harper Business, 2019).

22. Robert A. Hillman, *Principles of Contract Law* (St. Paul, MN: Thomson West, 2004); Barry D. Smith and Eric A. Wiening, *How Insurance Works* (Malvern, PA: American Institute for Chartered Property Casualty Underwriters/Insurance Institute of America, 1994); Harriet E. Jones and Dani L. Long, *Principles of Insurance: Life, Health, and Annuities* (Atlanta, GA: Life Office Management Association, 1999).

23. Paul N. Bloom and J. Gregory Dees, "Cultivate Your Ecosystem," *Stanford Social Innovation Review* (Winter 2008) (https://ssir.org/articles/entry/cultivate_your_ecosystem).

## Part IV

1. W. Edwards Deming, *Out of the Crisis* (Cambridge, MA: MIT Center for Advanced Engineering Study, 1986), 86.

## Chapter 8

1. Frederick Fungston and Stephen Wagner, *Surviving and Thriving in Uncertainty: Creating the Risk Intelligent Enterprise* (New York, NY: Wiley 2010), 277.

2. BoardSource, *The Nonprofit Board Answer Book: A Practical Guide for Board Members and Chief Executives* (San Francisco, CA: Jossey-Bass, 2011).

## Appendix 1

1. Kevin P. Kearns, "Accountability in the Nonprofit Sector," in Lester M. Salamon (ed.), *The State of Nonprofit America*, 2nd ed. (Washington, DC: Brookings Institution Press, 2012).
2. Ann Goggins Gregory and Don Howard, "The Nonprofit Starvation Cycle," *Stanford Social Innovation Review* (Fall 2009) (https://ssir.org/articles/entry/the_nonprofit_starvation_cycle).
3. Ellie Buteau, Andrea Brock, and Mark Chaffin, *Nonprofit Challenges: What Foundations Can Do* (Cambridge, MA: Center for Effective Philanthropy, 2013) (http://cep.org/wp-content/uploads/2016/08/NonprofitChallenges.pdf), 6.
4. Angela Francis and Jennifer Talansky, *Small Nonprofits Solving Big Problems* (New York, NY: Nonprofit Finance Fund, 2012) (https://nff.org/report/small-nonprofits-solving-big-problems), 10.
5. Kim Jonker and William F. Meehan III, "Fundamentals, Not Fads," *Stanford Social Innovation Review* (Spring 2014) (https://ssir.org/articles/entry/fundamentals_not_fads#:~:text=Fundamentals%2C%20Not%20Fads,%2C%20Funding%2C%20Leadership%2C%20etc.).
6. Nonprofit Finance Fund, *State of the Nonprofit Sector 2015 Survey* (New York, NY: Nonprofit Finance Fund, 2015) (available at https://nff.org/report/2015-state-sector-survey-brochure), 6.
7. Lester M. Salamon, "The Resilient Sector: The Future of Nonprofit America," in Lester M. Salamon (ed.), *The State of Nonprofit America*, 2nd ed. (Washington, DC: Brookings Institution Press, 2012), 47.
8. The Case Foundation, "The Pros and Cons of Working in the Nonprofit Sector," *The Case Foundation* (blog) (February 17, 2011) (https://casefoundation.org/blog/pros-and-cons-working-nonprofit-sector/).
9. Ibid.
10. Ibid.

11. Princeton Survey Research Associates, *Health of the Nonprofit, For-Profit, and Public Service Sectors* (February 15, 2002) (https://www.brookings.edu/wp-content/uploads/2016/06/NonprofitTopline.pdf).

12. Marla Cornelius and Patrick Corvington, "Nonprofit Workforce Dynamics," in Lester M. Salamon (ed.), *The State of Nonprofit America*, 2nd ed. (Washington, DC: Brookings Institution Press, 2012), 640.

13. Peter Bolton, "Nonprofit Employers Don't Meet Workers' Needs for Job Satisfaction, Surveys Find," *The Chronicle of Philanthropy* (blog) (October 24, 2011) (https://www.philanthropy.com/article/nonprofit-employers-dont-meet-workers-needs-for-job-satisfaction-surveys-find/).

14. "Job Satisfaction Up, Majority Still Not Thrilled" *The Nonprofit Times* (September 9, 2015) (https://www.thenonprofittimes.com/npt_articles/job-satisfaction-up-majority-still-not-thrilled/).

15. Marla Cornelius and Patrick Corvington, "Nonprofit Workforce Dynamics," 639. See also Rick Cohen, "Nonprofit Salaries: Achieving Parity with the Private Sector," *Nonprofit Quarterly* (June 21, 2010) (https://nonprofitquarterly.org/nonprofit-salaries-achieving-parity-with-the-private-sector/).

16. Peter Manzo, "The Real Salary Scandal," *Stanford Social Innovation Review* (Winter 2004) (https://ssir.org/articles/entry/the_real_salary_scandal).

17. David Garvey, "Nonprofit Sector: Workforce Education Needs and Opportunities," *Continuing Higher Education Review* 73 (Fall 2009): 114–124) (https://files.eric.ed.gov/fulltext/EJ903456.pdf).

18. Marla Cornelius and Patrick Corvington, "Nonprofit Workforce Dynamics," 645.

19. Opportunity Knocks, *Engaging the Nonprofit Workforce: Mission, Management and Emotion* (2011) (https://www.gcn.org/sites/default/files/ctools/OK_Engaging_the_Nonprofit_Workforce_Report.pdf), 12.

20. Libbie Landles-Cobb, Kirk Kramer, and Katie Smith Milway. "The Nonprofit Leadership Development Deficit," *Stanford Social Innovation Review* (October 22, 2015) (https://ssir.org/articles/entry/the_nonprofit_leadership_development_deficit).

21. David Larcker, Nicholas Donatiello, Bill Meehan, and Brian Tayan, *2015 Survey on Board of Directors of Nonprofit Organizations* (Stanford, CA: Stanford Graduate School of Business, 1996) (https://www.gsb .stanford.edu/sites/default/files/publication-pdf/cgri-survey-nonprofit-board-directors-2015.pdf).
22. Manda Salls, "Why Nonprofits Have a Board Problem," *Harvard Business School Working Knowledge* (blog) (April 4, 2005) (https:// hbswk.hbs.edu/archive/why-nonprofits-have-a-board-problem).
23. Alice Korngold, "Nonprofit Boards: On Saying No to Problem Board Members," *Fast Company* (blog) (March 18, 2011) (https://www .fastcompany.com/1739927/nonprofit-boards-saying-no-problem-board-members).
24. Criminal Justice Caucus at the Columbia School of Social Work, "Review of 'No One Wants to Work with Me: Working with Difficult Populations," *Criminal Justice Caucus* (blog) (April 17, 2012) (https:// criminaljusticecaucus.wordpress.com/2012/04/17/review-of-no-one-wants-to-work-with-me-working-with-difficult-populations-workshop/).
25. Salamon, "The Resilient Sector."
26. Dennis R. Young, Lester M. Salamon, and Mary Clark Grinsfelder, "Commercialization, Social Ventures, and For-Profit Competition," in Lester M. Salamon (ed.), *The State of Nonprofit America*, 2nd ed. (Washington, DC: Brookings Institution Press, 2012), 521.
27. Ibid.
28. Salamon, "The Resilient Sector."
29. Marla Cornelius and Patrick Corvington, "Nonprofit Workforce Dynamics."
30. Salamon, "The Resilient Sector," 34.
31. Ibid., 37.
32. Elizabeth Schmidt, "Rediagnosing 'Founder's Syndrome': Moving Beyond Stereotypes to Improve Nonprofit Performance," *Nonprofit Quarterly* (July 1, 2013) (https://nonprofitquarterly.org/rediagnosing-founder-s-syndrome-moving-beyond-stereotypes-to-improve-nonprofit-performance/).
33. Katie Smith Milway, Maria Orozco, and Christina Botero, "Why Nonprofit Mergers Continue to Lag," *Stanford Social Innovation*

*Review* (Spring 2014) (https://ssir.org/articles/entry/why_nonprofit_mergers_continue_to_lag).

34. The Hewlett Foundation, *The Nonprofit Marketplace: Bridging the Information Gap in Philanthropy* (2008) (https://hewlett.org/wp-content/uploads/2016/08/whitepaper.pdf).

35. Regina E. Herzlinger, "Effective Oversight," *Harvard Business Review on Nonprofits* (Cambridge, MA: Harvard Business Review, 1994), 42.

## Appendix 5

1. *Standards for Excellence®: An Ethics and Accountability Code for the Nonprofit Sector* (Baltimore, MD: Maryland Nonprofits, 2014) (https://standardsforexcellence.org/Home-2/code).

2. Ibid.

3. Nancy Bacon, "You Don't Get Compliance by Talking About Compliance," NancyBacon.com (blog) (October 5, 2021) (https://nancybacon.com/you-dont-get-compliance-by-talking-about-compliance/).

# About the Author

**Ted Bilich** founded Risk Alternatives LLC in 2013 with the mission of making communities stronger by building resilient, sustainable, agile nonprofits. Risk Alternatives helps nonprofits identify and manage their risks, address their most important challenges, and build a culture of continuous improvement.

Before founding Risk Alternatives, Ted was a Distinguished Visiting Professor from Practice at Georgetown University Law Center. Prior to that, Ted spent more than 20 years in the Washington, DC, office of an international law firm.

Ted is a Standards for Excellence® Licensed Consultant and is also a member of the National Standards for Excellence® Council. He has also served on the Arlington (Virginia) Economic Development Commission and the boards of numerous nonprofits. He is a member of the American Law Institute (ALI), the leading independent organization in the United States producing scholarly work to clarify, modernize, and improve the law. He served on the Member Consultative Group for the ALI's successful project on Principles of the Law, Compliance and Enforcement for Organizations.

Ted speaks regularly before large and small groups throughout the United States on risk management, board governance, civic engagement, ethics, and many other issues. He is also the author of three editions of a leading law school casebook on class actions and other multiparty dispute resolution. He received his BA in economics summa cum laude from Wake Forest University and his JD cum laude from Harvard Law School.

After spending much of his professional life in the Washington, D.C., area, Ted now resides with his wife and dog in Madison, Wisconsin.

# Index

NOTE: Page references in *italics* refer to figures.

## A

Abraham, Jay, 88

Accountability, 100–101

Action, for risk management, 20–21

Articles of incorporation, 175–176

Assessment and improvement, 95–127

  Lean Risk Management implementation for, 115–127 (*See also* Lean Risk Management implementation)

  risk management cycle for, 99–105 (*See also* Risk management cycle)

  working at board level for, 107–113 (*See also* Boards of directors)

Auditing vs. risk management, 23–24

Avoiding risk, 74, *74*, 80, 80–82. *See also* Response to risk

## B

Basel II accords (Basel Committee on Banking Supervision), 9

Boards of directors, 107–113

  asking questions about governance, 165–166

  challenges specific to nonprofits, 138–139

identifying stakeholders and
their interests, 119–120
risk dialectic and, 53–54
role in risk management,
107–113
sharing risk register
information with, 66
training, about risk
management, 125
BoardSource, 113
Book, organization of, 6, 13–14
Brookings Institute, 136
Brown, Tim, 90
Budget planning, 124–125

C
Challenges specific to
nonprofits
board issues, 138–139
competition, 141–142
compliance issues, 142
"market" failures, 143–145
planning and visioning
issues, 145–146
political worries, 142
service population
challenges, 140–141
volunteer challenges,
139–140
Check-in dates, 66, 68
The Checklist Manifesto
(Gawande), 86–87
Checklists
for compliance, 181–185
creating, 86–87, 86, 105

Childrens Community
Services, 10
Circles of Concern, Influence,
Control, 43
Clarity First (Martin), 46
Collaboration, 92
Commitment
risk inventory for, 38
to risk management, 20–21
Committee of Sponsoring
Organizations of the
Treadway Commission
(COSO), 9
Communication
board's role in setting tone for
organization, 110–113
discussing risk inventory with
team members, 38, 44, 55
email language, 47
feedback mechanisms/
records, 178–179
guarded, 133
"smooth sailing"
documents, 178
See also Meetings; Questions
Competition of nonprofits,
141–142
Compliance
challenges, 142
checklist for, 171–185
defined, 181–182
questions to ask
about, 162–163
Continuity plan, 178
Contracts, 92

Core procedural documents, 176–177
Covey, Stephen, 43
Crisis communication plan, 178
"Crystal ball" vs. risk management, 25–26
Customers
  Lean management for focus on, 31
  risk response and considering, 90
  soliciting insights from, 102
  testing risk management cycle among, 121
Cyber threats, 135

**D**
Deming, W. Edwards, 85, 88
Design thinking, 90
Development of opportunities, 74, *74*, 88–91, *88*. *See also* Response to risk
Development (sales to donors), 159–161
District of Columbia Bar, 8
Diversity, equity, and inclusion, 167
Documentation, 85, *85*–86, *99*. *See also* Communication; Fundamental risk management elements (FRaMEs)
Donors. *See* Funders
Drucker, Peter, 42

**E**
Email language, 47
Emotion, risk inventories and, 45–47
Enterprise Risk Management— Integrated Framework, 10
Error proofing, 87, *87*
Executives
  risk dialectic and, 53–54
  risk inventory for identifying participants, 39–40
  testing risk management cycle among, 122
External context, 167–170

**F**
Federation Employment and Guidance Service (FEGS), 10
Feedback
  from customers, 102
  mechanisms/records, 178–179
*Fierce Conversations* (Scott), 46
*The Fifth Discipline Fieldbook* (Senge), 46
Financial issues
  allocating resources, 117
  asking questions about, 152–155
  budget planning, 124–125
  challenges specific to nonprofits, 132–134
  funders and, 121–122
Fine, Allison, 15
Fishbone Diagram, 80

5 Whys methodology, 79
*The Flaw of Averages*
(Savage), 59
*Flow in the Office* (Venegas), 78
FMEA (Failure Mode and
Effects Analysis), 79, 91
Founder's syndrome, 143–144
Frontline personnel
testing risk management
cycle among, 121
training, about risk
management, 127
*See also* Team
Fundamental risk management
elements (FRaMEs), 14,
112, 175–179
Funders
donor base squeeze, 134
importance of risk
management for, 5
testing risk management
cycle among, 121–122
Fundraising, perpetual, 133
Fungston, Frederick, 108

**G**
Garry, Joan, 12–13
Gawande, Atul, 86–87
Goals, setting, 124
Goodwill Industries of
Toronto, 10
Governance. *See* Boards
of directors
Gregory, Ann Goggins, 133

**H**
Herzlinger, Regina, 145
Howard, Don, 133
*How to Measure Anything*
(Hubbard), 59
Hubbard, Douglas, 59
Human Services Council
of New York, 8–9

**I**
*The Improvement Guide*
(Langley), 88
Information, for risk
management, 20–21
Information technology,
151–152, 179
Insight and Exploration
about, 5
board's role in risk
management, 113
Lean Risk
Management, 32–33
response to risk, 93
risk inventory, 46–47
risk management,
overview, 14–16
risk management cycle, 105
timetable, 127
Inspection, 88, 88
Insurance
risk management
vs., 24–25, 91
types of, 179
Ishikawa, Kaoru, 80

**K**
Kanter, Beth, 15
Krafcik, John, 30

**L**
Langley, Gerald, 88
Leaders
  hidden tasks of nonprofit
    leaders, 11–13, 15
  importance of risk
    management for, 5 (*See
    also* Risk management)
  supplemental prioritization
    rubric, 56–58
Lean management principles
  Deming and, 84
  "stand in the circle," 79
Lean Risk Management, 17–33
  clarifying risk management,
    21–26, 26
  commitment, process,
    information,
    and action for, 20–21
  for continuous
    improvement, 129–130
  Insight and Exploration
    for, 32–33
  Lean Management movement
    and, 30–32
  risk, defined, 18–20
  risk inventory, risk register,
    risk cycle,
    defined, 26–30, 27
  risk management,
    defined, 19–20

  threats and opportunities,
    defined, 18, 19
  *See also* Assessment and
    improvement; Lean
    Risk Management
    implementation; Risk
    inventory; Risk register
Lean Risk Management imple-
    mentation, 115–127
  allocating resources, 117
  budget planning for, 124–125
  developing time line,
    116–117, 127
  identifying stakeholders and
    their interests, 119–122
  risk inventory process, 117–118
  risk management cycle
    testing, 118–119
  risk register development, 118
  setting goals for, 124
  shared vision for, 123
  training and, 126–127
Legal issues. *See* Compliance
Loss prevention, 19. *See also*
    Risk management

**M**
Management. *See* Senior staff
"Market" failures, 143–145
Martin, Karen, 32, 46, 86
Meetings
  frequency of, 98–99
  for reviewing risk register, 67
  risk inventory dialogue with
    team members, 38, 44, 55

sharing information about
    risk register,
    66, 101–102
Metrics. *See* Research and
    measurement
Miller, Jon, 30
Mistakes, learning from, 127
Mitigation, 82–88
    characteristics of
        impact and, 82
    checklists and, 86–87, 86
    defined, 74, 74, 82, 82
    documenting and, 85,
        85–86
    error proofing and, 87, 87
    inspecting and, 88, 88
    modifying activity that
        triggers risk, 84, 84
    objectives of impact and, 83
    as response to risk, 29
    standardizing and, 85, 85
    supervising and, 88, 88
    training and, 84, 84
    *See also* Response to risk; Risk
        management
Modifying activity, 84, 84
Monitoring, 29. *See also* Risk
    management
Monitoring response to risk, 74,
    75, 93, 93. *See also*
    Response to risk

N

Name, claim, record, celebrate
    (NCRC) value, 102–103

*New York Times*, 14
*The Nonprofit Board Answer
    Book* (BoardSource),
    113
Nonprofits, challenges
    of, 131–146
    financial, 132–134
    staffing and motivation,
        135–138
    technology, 134–135
    *See also* Challenges specific
        to nonprofits
Nonprofits Build Strength
    Together (BeST), 104
Non-value-adding activities,
    identifying, 42
"Nose in, hands off," 108
"No-vote" risks, 99–100

O

Operations, 147–151
Opportunities. *See* Threats
    and opportunities
Osterling, Mike, 32, 86
Ownership
    in for-profit organizations,
        52–53
    in nonprofit organizations,
        53–54
    risk inventory for, 38

P

Perspective, importance
    of, 101–102
Pilot programs, 88–89

Planning and visioning
  asking questions
    about, 163–165
  core planning documents,
    177
  mission creep, 134
  planning and visioning
    challenges, 145–146
  shared vision, 123
  standardization, 8–9, 85, 85
  strategic planning vs. risk
    management, 22–23
*Poka-yoke*, 87
Policy templates, 171–173. *See
  also* Rules
Political challenges, 142
Positive risk, developing,
  88–90, 88
Premortem exercise,
  79–80, 91
Principles & Practices for
  Nonprofit Excellence, 8
Prioritization, 49–69
  board's role in prioritizing risk
    management
    work, 109–110
  identifying stakeholders and
    their interests, 119–122,
    144–145
  risk management cycle
    for, 28, 100
  risk register for, 61–69 (*See
    also* Risk register)
  of risks, 51–59, *52*
  *See also* Challenges specific to
    nonprofits

ProBonoPartner.org, 183
Process
  process descriptions, 85–86
  for risk management, 20–21
Pryor, Robert, 85

**Q**
Questions
  asking, 76–77 (*See also*
    Research and
    measurement)
  compliance, 162–163
  diversity, equity,
    inclusion, 167
  external context, 167–170
  finance, 152–155
  governance, 165–166
  information technology,
    151–152
  operations, 147–151
  planning and visioning,
    163–165
  reputation management,
    157–158
  risk management, 161–162
  sales of goods/services,
    158–159
  sales to donors
    (development), 159–161
  talent management,
    155–157

**R**
Reflection/evaluation
  function, 109–110
Regulation. *See* Compliance

Reputation management,
    157–158
Research and measurement
  avoiding complex
      calculations for
      measurement, 58–59
  core metrics, 177–178
  research and response to
      risk, 74, 74, 76,
      76–80
  for threat cycle, 28–29
Resilience
  as goal, 3
  improving organizational
      resilience, 13–14
  Lean management for
      investing in, 32
Response to risk, 73–93
  addressing risk, overview,
      74, 74–76, 75
  avoiding risk and, 80,
      80–82
  development of opportunities
      and, 88–91, 88
  Insight and Exploration, 93
  mitigation and, 29, 82–85,
      82–88, 86–88
  monitoring, 93, 93
  research and, 76, 76–80
  risk management cycle for,
      28–29 (See also Risk
      management cycle)
  shifting risk and, 91,
      91–92

Risk Alternatives LLC, 9
Risk champions
  accountability of, 100–101
  roles of, 65–68
Risk dialectic, 52, 52–54
Risk inventory, 37–47
  benefits of, 38–39
  caveats for, 45–46
  defined, 27–30
  discussing with team
      members, 38, 44, 55
  for evaluating function in
      organization, 40, 40–43
  for identifying participants,
      39–40
  identifying threats/opportuni-
      ties in, 43–44, 46–47, 52
  Insight and
      Exploration, 46–47
  for positive and negative
      risks of, 39
  process of, 117–118
  questions to ask during,
      147–170 (See also
      Questions)
  simplifying process of, 43–44
  See also Risk register
Risk management, 1–33
  clarifying, 21–26, 26
  importance of, 3–16 (See also
      Risk management
      importance)
  language of, 17–33 (See also
      Lean risk management)

resilience as goal, 1
risk, defined, 18–20
*See also* Assessment and
    improvement;
    Communication;
    Compliance; Lean Risk
    Management;
    Prioritization;
    Response to risk
Risk management cycle,
    99–105
accountability and, 100–101
defined, 26–30, *27*, 98
developing support networks
    for, 104
identifying new risks, 100
Insight and Exploration, 105
inventory, register,
    and, 26–30
name, claim, record, celebrate
    (NCRC) value
    for, 102–103
"no-vote" risks as basis for
    work sessions, 99–100
prioritization and, 28, 100
reviewing risk register,
    98, 99
risk management discussion
    frequency, 98–99
soliciting perspectives
    for, 101–102
testing, 118–119
what's in it for them (WIIFT)
    and, 103–104

Risk management importance,
    3–16
book organization
    and, 6, 13–14
hidden tasks of nonprofit
    leaders, 11–13, 15
Insight and Exploration
    for, 14–16
new technologies as
    threats, 11
roles of nonprofits and, 4–5
standards and plans for risk
    management, 8–9
trust and, 9–11
vulnerability of nonprofits
    and, 7–8
Risk register, 61–69
appointing risk reporter, 63
check-in dates for, 68
defined, 27–30
developing, 118
identifying threats/opportuni-
    ties that were left out, 68
as key tool to Lean Risk
    Management, 62–63
people to share information
    with, 67
reviewing, 67
risk champions and,
    65–68, 100–101
risk reporters for, 63, 99
risk task force (RTF) for, 63
spreadsheets for, 64–66
uses for, 68

Risk tolerance, 111
Rules
  board's conduct and, 112–113
  core procedural documents,
    176–177
  policy templates, 171–173
  training frontline
    personnel, 126
  See also Compliance

S
SafetyCulture, 183
Sales of goods/services,
  158–159
Sales to donors (development),
  159–161
Savage, Sam, 59
Scarcity mindset, 133
Scott, Susan, 46
Securities Exchange
  Commission (US), 10
Senge, Peter, 46
Senior staff
  testing risk management
    cycle among senior staff,
    118–119, 120
  training, about risk
    management, 126
Service populations, challenges
  related to, 140–141
The Seven Habits of Highly
  Effective People
  (Covey), 43

Shared vision, 123. See also
  Planning and visioning
Shifting risk, 74, 74, 91, 91–92.
  See also Response to risk
Signposting, 86
The Smart Nonprofit (Kanter
  and Fine), 15
"smooth sailing" documents,
  178
Social services nonprofits,
  vulnerability of, 7–8
Spreadsheets, populating,
  64–66
Standardization, 8–9, 85, 85
Standards for Excellence
  Institute, 8
"Stand in the circle," 79
Stanford Social Innovation
  Review, 133
Starvation cycle, 133
Strategic planning vs. risk
  management, 22–23
Successes, capturing,
  102–103
Succession plan, 178
Supervision, 88, 88
Supplemental prioritization
  rubric, 56–58
Support networks, 104
Surviving and Thriving in
  Uncertainty (Fungston
  and Wagner), 108
Systems thinking, 90

**T**

Taleb, Nassim Nicholas, 80

Talent management, 155–157

Team

board's knowledge that team is performing risk management work, 108–109

challenges specific to nonprofits, 135–138

identifying functions of (*See* Risk inventory)

Lean management for energizing, 31

risk dialectic and, 53–54

risk inventory discussions with, 55

sharing risk register information with, 67, 101–102

staffing and motivation challenges, 135–138

supervision, *88, 88*

testing risk management cycle among senior staff, 118–119

training, *84, 84*–85

*See also* Meetings; Risk management cycle

Technology

asking questions about, 151–152

challenges specific to nonprofits, 134–135

new technologies as threats, 11

Threats and opportunities

"crystal ball" *vs.* risk management, 25–26

defined, *18, 19*

identifying top three threats (*See* Risk inventory)

internal nature of, 32

risk register for identifying, 68

soliciting perspectives about, 102

*See also* Challenges specific to nonprofits

Time line, 116–117, 127. *See also* Lean Risk Management implementation

Toyoda, Sakichi, 79

Toyota Motor Company, 30, 79

Training, *84, 84,* 125–127, 137

Trust, risk management importance and, 9–11

**U**

Utah Food Bank, 11

**V**

*Value Stream Mapping* (Martin and Osterling), 32, 86

Venegas, Carlos, 42, 78

Vision. *See* Planning and visioning

Visual signposting, 86

Volunteer challenges, 139–140

Vulnerability of nonprofits, 7–8

**W**
Wagner, Stephen, 108
*Washington Post*, 11
What's in it for them
     (WIIFT), 103–104

Wickman, Gino, 86
Worrying vs. risk
     management, 21
Wounded Warrior
     Project Fund, 10